COURSEWORK

MATHEMATICS

Investigations and problem solving activities

Keith Sharp

Deputy Head
William de Ferrers School
Essex

Ian Wilson

Deputy Head
Park Barn School
Guildford

UNWIN HYMAN

First published 1987 by Unwin Hyman Limited
15–17 Broadwick Street
London W1V 1FP

Reprinted 1988

Acknowledgements
We are grateful to the long-suffering pupils of West Hatch
High School and William Ellis School, who enthusiastically
tried out these activities. We are sorry that we could only
include a small sample of the work they produced. Our
colleagues in the mathematics departments of the two schools
provided invaluable comments and support, and thanks are
due to them. Above all, a special thanks to Deborah and
Barbara.

Cover and pupils' pages illustrated by Charles Snape.

ISBN 0 7135 2812 5

Typeset by MS Filmsetting Limited, Frome, Somerset
Printed in Great Britain by Bell & Bain Ltd, Glasgow
Bound by Hunter & Foulis Ltd, Edinburgh

Contents

Teachers' guide

Introduction

This collection of 42 investigations and practical problem-solving activities with comprehensive teaching notes has been designed
— to help teachers new to this type of work
— to enrich any mathematics course
— to provide material for classes taking GCSE courses.

The activities will supplement any mathematics course and can be used in several ways: to consolidate other work, as an independent element of the course, or as a way of introducing new content.

From 1991, all GCSE examinations will include an element of coursework. The authors, both experienced mathematics teachers, felt that there was a shortage of suitable materials for teachers faced with the task of preparing pupils for these examinations. The ideas have been tested in classrooms and there are enough of them to cover the normal range of ability and ages found in secondary schools. The teachers' notes give guidance on each task, including materials required, and ideas for extension work where appropriate. We have also included some questions which may help in assessing pupils' work. For these we have used a simplified version of the criteria used by the examination boards. These are not intended to be definitive, but to identify the key points which will form the major part of the assessment process.

Many teachers may be wary of embarking on a method of teaching which is strange to them, and where it seems that they have little control over pupils' actions, but we would encourage them to persist, because the increased motivation and confidence of pupils are well worth the effort. It is for this reason that we have used these activities. By working in this way, pupils develop mathematical strategies for themselves. Strategies such as generalising, inventing their own notation, testing ideas, and making deductions may all form part of the pupils' individual approaches to these tasks. They 'own' their mathematics in a way not always possible in conventional teaching.

Why investigations?

Recent years have seen a greater interest in the development of mathematical processes in students. The reasons for this are many, but we can certainly point to the impetus given by research projects which have demonstrated that pupils learn best when actively involved in mathematics. The Cockcroft report stated, "The idea of investigation is fundamental both to the study of mathematics itself and also to an understanding of the ways in which mathematics can be used to extend knowledge and to solve problems in very many fields" (para. 250). Investigational work was suggested as one of the techniques that should be used in mathematics teaching at all levels (para 243), and the report further endorsed the idea in paragraph 322: "Mathematical exploration and investigations are of value even when they are not directed specifically to the learning of new concepts".

Some GCSE syllabuses already include an element of coursework, and in many cases this takes the form of investigations and the solving of practical problems. From 1991, all syllabuses will have to include coursework and this means that many schools will now be considering how to introduce pupils in the lower school to these ideas, in preparation for GCSE. Paragraph 2.13 of the National Criteria states that courses should enable pupils to "develop their mathematical abilities by considering problems and conducting individual and cooperative enquiry and experiment, including extended pieces of work of a practical and investigative kind". The tasks in this book will be useful both in schools preparing for these changes and in those which are already using such courses.

The skills and processes which are used in tackling investigative work will, of course, vary with the problem, but are likely to include:

> recognising the problem
> searching for patterns
> tabulation
> inventing notation
> developing hypotheses
> testing hypotheses
> making generalisations
> proving results
> communicating results

Investigations can thus be seen as important not just because of the mathematical content which they use, but because they give practice in developing skills and processes.

How to use the activities

In the teaching notes we have suggested ways in which you could use the tasks and have tried to anticipate, from our own experience, the guidance you will need to provide, but in order for you to be of most help to your pupils, we strongly urge you to try each of the activities before doing them with a class. In this way you will know some of the directions which may be taken by the pupils, and can anticipate 'sticking points' which might occur. Pupils should be allowed sufficient time to explore the situation and, if necessary, discuss it with other pupils. They will often get stuck up blind alleys — but don't be tempted to intervene too much. Suggestions like "Have you thought of...", "What if...", can be used sparingly in the initial stage. Your role in the lesson will clearly be different to the one you have in conventional teaching. Circulating around the class, promoting discussion, and guiding those who lack self-confidence are all methods you will employ. At times we have been confronted with questions we did not anticipate or results we had not found and it is exciting (and unsettling!) to be able to say "I don't know. Let's find out..." Certain techniques such as tabulating, keeping one variable fixed, or simplifying the problem are very useful in many investigations, and pupils will soon become proficient with them.

You should emphasise the need for accuracy and for checking results. Pupils often jump to conclusions too quickly and you will need to encourage them to try their theories with new examples in order to test them. Proving results can often be difficult but verbal and written explanations are equally acceptable, particularly from younger pupils who may lack algebraic or other knowledge. Pupils should also be encouraged to get into the habit of keeping working notes. Writing up the results is an important part of the activity, but pupils will not find this easy at first. You will need to explain that you will want to see all their working and their thinking, aiming for completeness without writing a novel! A possible model for a report is:

(a) What is the problem about?
(b) How did you start?
(c) How did you go on?
(d) What examples did you try?
(e) Did you have any theories, right or wrong?
(f) If you had to give up an idea, why did you?
(g) What did you try next, and why?
(h) Any final conclusions?
(i) Any ideas for possible extensions?

The activities vary in the time needed to complete them. For longer investigations, a lesson in class could be followed by the pupils completing the task as a project, to be handed in at a later date. It will be useful during this time to have occasions when the pupils' work can be pulled together and discussed.

The activities are in no particular order, but the contents grid will give you an indication of the age range and topics covered. You can therefore use the tasks in a flexible way.

Assessment

We are often asked, by teachers new to using investigative work, how to assess pupils' work. It does need a different approach, because pupils often find it difficult, especially at first, to write up their results, let alone clearly explain how they explored the situation and what were their lines of thought. Indeed, since much of the purpose of this work is to develop mathematical processes, a great deal of your assessment will be in observing how your pupils tackle the problems and what strategies they use. Most of the assessment will thus be formative, designed to provide information on the pupils' mathematical development and also to provide them with feedback. The extent to which pupils' work is assessed will clearly vary, with work done in the later years of a GCSE course needing to be more thoroughly examined, and summative assessment will then be important. We return to this later.

Some investigations are more closed than others and it is relatively easy to check if pupils have succeeded, but many will lead to widely differing results being handed in, and it then becomes important to check the processes which have been used. We have used the following criteria as the main framework for our assessment guidelines: comprehension; planning; searching for patterns; generalising; testing hypotheses and proving results; and, finally, presenting arguments and communicating results. We have applied this framework to each of the investigations and identified the main areas to be considered. We pose suitable questions to help assess pupils' work and these appear at the end of the relevant teachers' notes. You will see that the areas we have singled out to be assessed differ from task to task. For example, in *Flickering Lights*, planning, generalising and testing hypotheses are particularly important, while the criteria highlighted in *It's a Gas* are comprehension and planning. We wish to emphasise however that our questions are *examples* of the sort which you should ask, and are there to help you become proficient in constructing your own sets of guidelines. If, for example, a pupil produces a generalisation which we have not specifically listed, he/she deserves to be credited with it, not penalised!

We have listed questions related to the presentation of results only when this is an important aspect of the investigation. Clarity of communication, neatness, and precision are obviously areas which are common to all the tasks.

We have tried to produce positive statements of the processes and results which are assessed, but these are not definitive and you may want to include others such as independence, creativity and perseverance.

Comprehension

Has the pupil understood what he/she has to do?
Has he/she identified the key factors?
Has he/she formed useful sub-problems to help solve the task?

Planning

Did the pupil have a strategy for carrying out the investigation?
Did the pupil use a suitable method?
Has the pupil used a systematic approach?

Searching for patterns

Has the pupil used techniques such as tabulating which would help in making patterns clearer?
Has the pupil generated sufficient examples to enable patterns to emerge?

Generalising

Has the pupil tried to generalise?
Has the pupil expressed the generalisations in words or in symbols?

Testing hypotheses and proving results

Has the pupil tried new examples to test his/her hypotheses?
Has the pupil attempted to prove his/her results?

Presenting arguments and communicating results

Has the pupil clearly explained what he/she has done at each stage?
Has the pupil produced a clear concise account of the investigation?
Has the pupil used diagrams, tables, etc where appropriate?
Has the pupil produced a report with a logical structure?

To show how these frameworks can be used, we have applied them to some pupils' work on *Flickering Lights* and *Snakes and Ladders*, in order to provide a formative assessment. This obviously is related to the particular pupils involved, but we hope it will show you what is possible.

(a) Robert Collis plus typescript (all one group)

Flickering Lights

Which lights will be left on if there are only 10 lights?

Step

1) lights:	1	2	3	4	5	6	7	8	9	10	are on
2) lights:	1		3		5		7		9		are on.
3) lights:	1				5	6	7				are on
4) lights:	1			4	5	6	7	8			are on.
5) lights:	1			4		6	7	8		10	are on
6) lights:	1			4			7	8		10	are on
7) lights:	1			4				8		10	are on
8) lights:	1			4						10	are on
9) lights:	1			4					9	10	are on
10) lights:	1			4					9		are on

If there are 10 lights, only lights 1, 4 and 9 will be left on after the 10 steps have been carried out.

Which lights will be left on if there are 20 lights?

Step   lights on.

	1	2	3	4	5	6	7	8	9	10	11	12	13	14	15	16	17	18	19	20
1)	1	2	3	4	5	6	7	8	9	10	11	12	13	14	15	16	17	18	19	20
2)	1		3		5		7		9		11		13		15		17		19	
3)	1				5	6	7				11	12	13				17	18	19	
4)	1			4	5	6	7	8			11		13			16	17	18	19	20
5)	1			4		6	7	8		10	11		13		15	16	17	18	19	
6)	1			4			7	8		10	11	12	13		15	16	17		19	
7)	1			4				8		10	11	12	13	14	15	16	17		19	
8)	1			4						10	11	12	13	14	15		17		19	
9)	1			4					9	10	11	12	13	14	15		17	18	19	
10)	1			4					9		11	12	13	14	15		17	18	19	20
11)	1			4					9			12	13	14	15		17	18	19	20
12)	1			4					9				13	14	15		17	18	19	20
13)	1			4					9					14	15		17	18	19	20
14)	1			4					9						15		17	18	19	20
15)	1			4					9								17	18	19	20
16)	1			4					9							16	17	18	19	20
17)	1			4					9							16		18	19	20
18)	1			4					9							16			19	20
19)	1			4					9							16				20
20)	1			4					9							16				

If there are 20 lights, the lights 1, 4, 9 and 16 are left on after the 20 steps have been carried out

In both examples after the steps have been carried out only the square numbers remain on.

Using this theory, if there are 1000 lights all the square numbers between 1 and 1000 will be left on after the 1000 steps have been carried out.

Thus would mean that:

31 lights would be left on

969 lights would be off.

On examining this problem we found that the best results would be obtained by working in a group.

In our group we manually constructed a table of results for differents sequences of lights. We experimented with multiples of ten lights and we noticed a pattern.

To prove this theory we decided to write a computer program to calculate the results for larger amounts of lights. This program was designed to allow the user to enter any amount of lights (up to a thousand) and receive the results in the form of screeen displays and a printout.

TYPE IN NO. LIGHTS =100
Please wait

     FOR Mr Sharp
      By Stephen Olney, Richard Bailey, Robert Collis & Anthony Taylor

The 1's stand for an ON light and the 0's stand for an OFF light.

10010000100000010000000010000000000100000000000010000000000000001000000
00000000000100000000000000000001

These are the lights that will be on after the 100 programs have been run :

LIGHT NO. = 1
LIGHT NO. = 4
LIGHT NO. = 9
LIGHT NO. = 16
LIGHT NO. = 25
LIGHT NO. = 36
LIGHT NO. = 49
LIGHT NO. = 64
LIGHT NO. = 81
LIGHT NO. = 100

This example gives us an answer to the investigation about the pier lighting scheme. The series of numbers that you can see represents the state of the lights after the 100 computer programs have been run.

The answer shows us that after the 100 programs have been run, the only lights that remain on are the SQUARE NUMBERS!

The lights that will be left on after the 1000 programs have been run will be :-

LIGHT NOS> =>
1,4,9,16,25,36,49,64,81,100,121,144,169,196,225,256,289,324,361,400,
441,484,529,576,625,676,729,784,841,900,961

WILL BE ON AND THESE ARE ALL SQUARE NUMBERS!

Flickering Lights

```
10INPUT"TYPE IN NO. LIGHTS" NO
20DIM A$(1000)
30FOR I=1 TO NO
40A$(I)="1"
50NEXT I
60PRINT"Please Wait"
70FOR OUTER=2 TO NO
80FOR INNER=1 TO NO STEP OUTER
90IF A$(INNER)="0"THEN A$(INNER)="1"ELSE IF A$(INNER)="1"THEN A$(INNER)="0"
100NEXT
110NEXT
120VDU14
130VDU14
150PRINT
160PRINT"     FOR Mr Sharp"
170PRINT"     By Stephen Olney, Richard Bailey, Robert Collis & Anthony Taylor
180PRINT:PRINT"The 1's stand for an ON light and the 0's stand for an OFF light"
190 PRINT
200VDU14
210FOR S=2 TO NO
220PRINTA$(S);
230NEXT S
240PRINT:PRINT:PRINT"These are the lights that will be on after the 100 programs have been run :"
250 PRINT:PRINT
260FOR N=1 TO NO
270IF N*N>NO THEN END
280PRINT "LIGHT NO. =";N*N
290NEXT N
```

(b) Ruth Johnson

Maths Investigation

~ Flickering Lights

A seaside town has just invested in 1000 new lights to illuminate the pier. They are all numbered from 1 to 1000, and linked to a computerised system which can turn on and off any single light. 1000 computer programs are used

The first program switches all the lights on
The second program switches off all the even numbered lights.
The third program will change the state of all the lights whose numbers are multiples of three (i.e. if they are off, it turns them on, and vice versa)
The fourth program will change the state of all the lights whose numbers are multiples of three (i.e. if they a
And so on.....

(1) Which lights will be on after the lights have been subjected to the 1000 different programs? Hint: it will probably be easier to work on a model using smaller numbers first.

(2) After the manager's experiment how many lights will be on? And how many will be off?

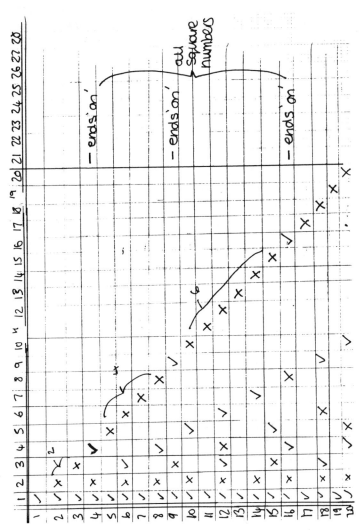

I used a model of 20 computer programmes and 20 lights. By working through the programmes I found that all the square numbers (eg 4, 9, 16 etc) were left on. This lights would still be left on even if 1000 computer programmes were used since after you have past that number it is not affected again.
This is how many programmes are affected with each computer programme

1st — all
2nd — half
3rd — 1/3
4th — 1/4
5th — 1/5
6th — 1/6
......
1000th — 1/1000 — only the number 1000

but how do you prove that every square number to 1000 stays on; well either test it! or pick numbers randomly to check.
Say; 12 , 56, 16, and 1000

12 - 1, 2, 3, 4, 6, 12 ← factors '6'
   ↓ ↓ ↓ ↓ ↓ ↓
   on off on off on off ← ends 'off'

56 - 1, 2, 4, 7, 8, 14, 28, 56 ← factors '8'
   ↓ ↓ ↓ ↓ ↓ ↓ ↓ ↓
   on off on off on off on off ← ends 'off'

16 - 1, 2, 4, 8, 16 ← factors '5' (odd no)
   ↓ ↓ ↓ ↓ ↓
   on off on off on ← ends 'on'

computer prog

↯	1	2	3	4	5	6	7	8	9	10
1	✓									
2	✓	✗								
3	✓		✗							
4	✓	✗		✓						
5	✓				✗					
6	✓	✗	✓			✗				
7	✓						✗			
8	✓	✗		✓				✗		
9	✓		✗						✓	
10	✓	✗		✓						✗

1000
factors
- 1, 2, 4, 5, 8, 10, 20, 25, 40, 50, 100, 125, 200, 250, 500, 1000
↓ ↓ ↓ ↓ ↓ ↓ ↓ ↓ ↓ ↓ ↓ ↓ ↓ ↓ ↓ ↓
1000 500 250 125 100 50 40 25 20 20 10 8 5 4 2 1
n° of lights affected by each programme

So if a multiple has an odd number of factors then it is a square number and the light will stay 'on'.

Number of square numbers in a thousand

1, 4, 9, 16, 25, 36, 49, 64, 81, 100, 121, 132, 169, 196, 225, 256, 289) . . . . . .

8 or $\sqrt{1000}$ = 31.62

31.6 'on' = 968.4 'off'

Given the abilities of the pupils who attempted this task, their results are of a good standard. It was particularly encouraging to see the group of boys working cooperatively on a slightly different approach to this task — and it was their own decision to work with the computer.

(c) Justin Kelly

<u>Snakes and Ladders : Investigation</u>

Ladder vector $\binom{2}{6}$

The mappings from this ladder are:

1 → 63	20 → 78	21 → 83
2 → 64	19 → 77	22 → 84
3 → 65	18 → 76	23 → 85
4 → 66	17 → 75	24 → 86
5 → 67	16 → 74	25 → 87
6 → 68	15 → 73	26 → 88
7 → 69	14 → 72	27 → 89
8 → 70	13 → 71	28 → 90

+62   +58   +62

If you move up this ladder from a line whose first number on the left is odd then you add 62 to your score
If the first number on the left is even then you add 58 to your score

This ladder can only be used from the first 4 lines because it reaches above the top line if you try to go any further. So the lines that you use '+62' on are the first and third, and when on the second or fourth you add 58.

The two different equations for this ladder are :

If moving from lines 1 or 3 you multiply the bottom number of the vector by 10 and add the top number
So for the vector $\binom{2}{6}$ it's,

$$(6 \times 10) + 2 + X \qquad \text{X = Number you start from (base of ladder)}$$

If moving from lines 2 or 4 you still multiply the bottom number by 10 but instead of adding the top number you subtract it,

$$(6 \times 10) - 2 + X$$

To work out the addition to your score using a ladder of any vector you use one of the following equations

$$\binom{X}{Y} = \text{top number}$$
$$= \text{bottom number}$$

odd number line (1, 3, 5), bottom number even

$$(Y \times 10) + X$$

even number line (2, 4, 6), bottom number even

$$(Y \times 10) - X$$

Odd number line, bottom number odd

$$(Y \times 10) + (X + Z)$$

even number line, bottom number odd

$$(Y \times 10) + (-X + -Z)$$

X	Z
2	+5
3	+3
4	+1
5	-1
6	-3
7	-5
8	-7
9	-9

(d) Marcel Ridyard

<u>Snakes and ladders.</u>   2/6/87

1) The vector of my ladder is, $\binom{2}{6}$

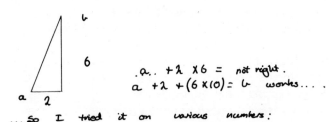

I have to find the relationship between the number at the bottom of the ladder and the one at the top when the ladder is moved around.

Here are all the different numbers I got.
a = base of ladder
b = top

a → b	a → b	a → b	a → b
1 → 63	13 → 71	21 → 83	33 → 91
2 → 64	14 → 72	22 → 84	34 → 92
3 → 65	15 → 73	23 → 85	35 → 93
4 → 66	16 → 74	24 → 86	36 → 94
5 → 67	17 → 75	25 → 87	37 → 95
6 → 68	18 → 76	26 → 88	38 → 96
7 → 69	19 → 77	27 → 89	39 → 97
8 → 70	20 → 78	28 → 90	40 → 98
+62	+58	+62	+58
+58			

∴ a + 62 = b when bottom numbers go up from left to right. (eg. 1 2 3 4 5 6 7 8 9 10)
a + 58 = b when numbers go from right to left.
(eg. 20 19 18 17 16 15 14 13 12 11)

I knew there had to be a relationship between the vector and the numbers a and b.

$$a + 2 \times 6 = \text{not right.}$$
$$a + 2 + (6 \times 10) = b \text{ works....}$$

... So I tried it on various numbers:

$$8 + 2 + (6 \times 10) = b$$
$$10 + 60 = 70 \qquad \text{yes !}$$

$$15 + 2 + (6 \times 10) = b$$
$$17 + 60 = 77 \qquad \text{no !}$$
it should be 73.

I looked back and saw that there must be two different fomuli. One for the numbers going from left to right and another for the numbers going from right to left.

So for going from left to right the formular is:

$$a + (6 \times 10) + 2 \qquad \longrightarrow$$

and for the opposite direction

$$a + (6 \times 10) - 2. \qquad \longleftarrow$$

$$15 + 60 - 2 = 73 \qquad \checkmark \text{ correct.}$$

	Marcel Ridyard	Justin Kelly	Olney, Bailey Collis, Taylor	Ruth Johnson
Comprehension	Good. Understood vectors and mappings.	Good. Understood vectors and mappings.	Good.	Good.
Planning	Good. Moved ladder in a systematic way.	Good. Moved ladder in a systematic way.	Good. Written sheet shows smaller number used plus table.	Good. Tried smaller numbers and tabulated results.
Searching for patterns	Good. Systematic recording. Results tabulated.	Good. Systematic recording. Results tabulated.		
Generalising	Reasonable. Has generalised for vector $\begin{pmatrix} 2 \\ 6 \end{pmatrix}$.	Reasonable. Has generalised for vector $\begin{pmatrix} 2 \\ 6 \end{pmatrix}$. Attempted more, but wrongly.	Reasonable. Recognised square numbers (not albebraic).	Good. Recognised square numbers (not algebraic).
Testing hypotheses	Reasonable. Has tested formula with one result.	Poor. Has not checked any of his generalisations.	Reasonable. Tested results but did not explain them.	Good. Tested and explained using factors. (N.B. slight error in factor diagram.)
Presenting results	Reasonable. Clear, fairly good explanation.	Poor. Not clear on what he was doing. Has not explained his 'odd/even' lines very well.	Good. Clear, concise, unusual.	Good. Main points highlighted. Well explained. Conclusion weak.
Observations	Only tried one ladder. Work done in 1 hour period, written up at home.	Has attempted to generalise for vector $\begin{pmatrix} a \\ b \end{pmatrix}$	Worked well as a group. Cooperated on writing program. High level of engagement with task. Virtually no teacher direction needed.	Worked alone. No teacher direction needed. Could give verbal explanation of what she had done.

In assessing the work of pupils of different abilities, you will need to use your professional judgement as to how much their work represents an achievement in developing their own individual mathematical potential, and the best way to encourage its further development. You will need to feed back your comments carefully to your pupils, so that they can build up their confidence in using the processes involved. Displaying pupils' work is of course a useful and pleasing way of providing reinforcement.

When it is necessary to assess pupils' work relative to each other, or for summative purposes (at the end of a course for example), a technique which we have found useful is to mark the work according to a weighted selection from the criteria which we have supplied. This implies some proficiency in using them in the way described above.

For the *Flickering Lights* task, such a scheme could look like this:

Comprehension	Planning	Generalising	Testing hyp.	Presentation	Discretionary*
2	3	6	4	2	3

Total 20

* Creativity, independence, etc.

For GCSE purposes, some examination groups provide detailed marking schemes, others merely provide guidelines. In constructing your own scheme, all the teachers involved should draw up their own weightings, then reach a consensus on the final scheme. The teachers should then assess the same five or six pieces of work according to the suggested scheme and discuss their marking together, before finally agreeing on a common interpretation of the scheme.

Teachers' notes

Introduction

This task is suitable for any age group and for individual or group work. It has great scope for cross-curricular links with other subject areas such as social studies, geography, art and design. It can equally stand on its own as an extended piece of work.

The problem is realistic, based on an actual housing development in Essex. The uniqueness of the housing design was probably inspired by the shape of the original plot and the location of the access roads.

You will probably wish to use this as a project that will require the pupils to do research into the social and mathematical aspects of this activity.

Equipment

Cut-out house and the site plan (a photocopy master is supplied at the end of this book). Scissors, calculators, coloured pencils, rulers, tracing paper.

Running the investigation

Initially a discussion about layouts of estates and the need for access and common areas, etc will stimulate ideas. This could be followed up by pupils in smaller groups 'brainstorming' the task.

As this is an extended piece of work, we suggest that after the initial session you return to the task at frequent intervals over a period of time, rather than trying to tackle it in consecutive sessions.

The quality of the pupil's final report is just as important as the design of the estate, and some pupils may need help and guidance on this. As well as a written account, the report could also include models, photographs and diagrams.

Assessment

Comprehension

Are all the houses of the same design?

Planning

Has the pupil included 32 houses?
Has the pupil included access roads?
Has the pupil included access to the houses?
Has the pupil tried to improve on her earlier attempts?
Has the pupil got a balance between housing and other amenities?
Has the pupil allowed for car parking and garage spaces?
Has the pupil considered the security aspect?

Presenting results

Has the pupil listed the advantages of his design?
Has the pupil listed the disadvantages of her design?
Is the drawing to scale?
Has the pupil identified the feature of his design by labels or a key?
Has the pupil included the approximate area of housing, garages, etc?

This is the actual site plan.

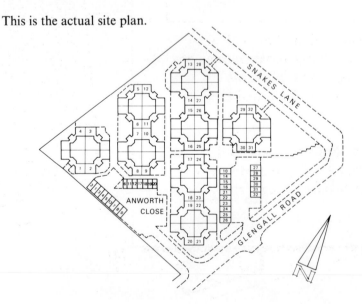

Architect's Dilemma

Within the marked out building site, you have been given planning permission to build 32 houses.

Your architect has chosen an unusual design for each of the houses:

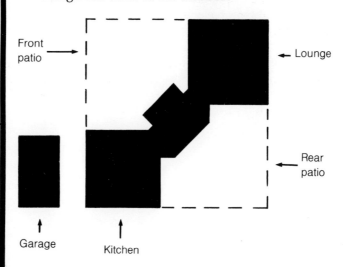

Front patio → ← Lounge ← Rear patio ↑ Garage ↑ Kitchen

Each house has the same design, but the front patio area can vary in size.

▶ Design a housing estate that would make the best use of the area and be a place where you would like to live.

Don't forget you will need to think about garages for each house, parking, common recreation areas, central bin areas, access from the main roads, and access to the houses.

Write a report on the good and bad aspects of your design, including the approximate areas used for houses, garages etc.

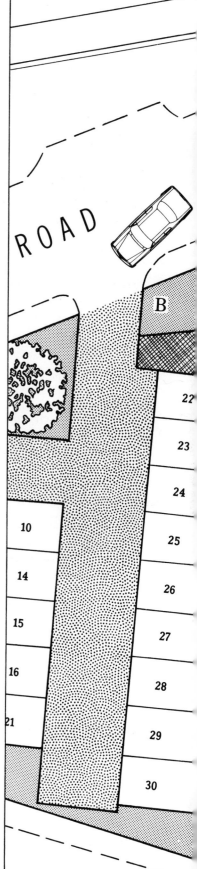

Teachers' notes

Introduction

Suitable for upper secondary pupils. This investigation should take about two teaching sessions to complete. Pupils will need to be familiar with trigonometry, areas of sectors, lengths of sectors, and perimeters. This task will help to reinforce these concepts and also gives the pupils the opportunity to write up and display their mathematics effectively.

Equipment

Using counters or coins would help most pupils' understanding of this task. Calculators will also be needed.

Running the investigation

This task will require a short explanation on the overhead projector, perhaps using three counters as an example, to revise some of the concepts involved. Pupils should then work on the task individually, and after some time be brought together as a group to discuss their answers to the first part.

Answers

1   $12 + 2\pi$ units
2   Area is $4\sqrt{3} + 12 + \pi$ sq. units
3   $12 + 2\pi$ units
4   $12 + \pi + 6\sqrt{3}$

Pupils should notice that the perimeter of the triangle shape is the same as that of the hexagonal display.

Assessment

Comprehension

Did the pupil understand that the band followed the contours of the tyres at the corners of the shape?
Did the pupil understand that the tangent to the circle meets the radius at 90°?

Planning

Did the pupil first look at smaller models?
Has the pupil used diagrams effectively to help solve the problem?
Has the pupil split the task up into smaller steps?

Searching for patterns

Has the pupil noticed that the perimeter of triangular shapes increases by 6 each time, e.g. $6 + 2\pi$, $12 + 2\pi$, etc?
Did the pupil notice that the area of the corners is one-third of the area of a circle in a triangular display, and one-sixth of the area of a circle in an hexagonal display?

Generalising

Has the pupil found the formula for the perimeter of a triangle, i.e. $6(n-1) + 2\pi$ for n tyres on each side (i.e. a total of $n(n+1)/2$ tyres)?

Presenting results

Has the pupil given specific results of perimeters and inside areas of all configurations?

The band

A tyre company wants to make a floor display of their new tyres.

For security reasons the tyres are bound together by an expensive special banding.

The manager decides to look at different configurations with 6 tyres.

His first attempt looks like this:

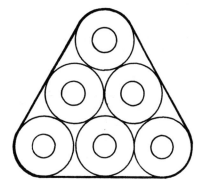

Assume that each tyre has a radius of 1 unit.

1. What would be the length of the banding required to wrap around the above display of tyres?

2. If the tyres were removed, what would be the area inside the banding?

The manager now decides to arrange the tyres in the form of a hexagon.

3. What would be the length of the band needed to go around the tyres?

4. What is the area inside the banding?

What do you notice?

▶Investigate other ways the 6 tyres could be arranged.

▶Investigate what happens if 3 tyres and if 10 tyres are arranged in triangular displays.

Teachers' notes

Introduction

This investigation can be successfully attempted by pupils of all ages, but only the more able will generalise the results. Working in pairs will help with the collection of results.

It can be used as an introduction to arrangements and to the idea of factorial notation.

Equipment

Prepared sheets with the relevant numbers of points on a circle should be handed out. These can be obtained commercially*, or can be easily prepared.

Running the investigation

Pupils should soon be able to detect a pattern and realise that they have to be careful not to count patterns twice. Some pupils may tackle the investigation by lettering the players and listing the possible orders.

Possible extensions

A different rule for passing the ball.

Answers

1 6 patterns
2 24 patterns
3 $(n-1)!$

Assessment

Comprehension

Has the pupil realised that the ball can be handled once only and that it must start and finish with the same player?

Planning

Has the pupil shown evidence of a strategy for finding the patterns?

Searching for patterns

Has the pupil made a table of the results?
Has the pupil seen a sequence in the tabulated results of different numbers of players?

Generalising

Has the pupil found that the number of patterns is $(n-1)!$?

Presenting results

Was the pupil able to explain the results even if she could not produce a formula, e.g. "the first player has 4 choices, the next player 3 choices, ..."?

*E.g. Gridsheets from Excitement in Learning, Mint Street, London SE1.

BASKETBALL ROUTINES

4 basketball players start a warm-up routine by standing on the circumference of a circle and passing the ball to each other.

The players are equally spaced around the circle.

The ball must start and finish with the same player and be handled by each of the players only once.

Investigate the different patterns that can be made by the path of the ball when ...

1.   4 players are playing

2.   5 players are playing

3.   Can you find how many patterns there are if n players are warming up?

Teachers' notes

Introduction

This is suitable for middle secondary school pupils. It is likely to take about one session of teaching time, and is an activity which requires no prior knowledge.

Most pupils will be able to draw suitable diagrams to answer the questions and to see the patterns required for generalising.

Equipment

Rulers; squared or plain paper.

Running the investigation

Pupils should have little problem starting the task, and should work individually.

When the number of cuts increases, pupils will find it difficult to count the number of pieces unless they adopt a strategy something like this:

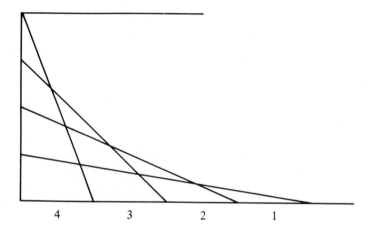

Answers

1 7 pieces
2 11 pieces
3 46 pieces

The formula for n cuts is $\frac{1}{2}n(n+1)+1$.

Assessment

Comprehension

Has the pupil realised that each cut must cross every other cut to produce the maximum number of pieces?

Planning

Has the pupil drawn clear, useful, diagrams?

Searching for patterns

Has the pupil considered consecutive numbers of cuts?
Has the pupil tabulated his results?

Generalising

Has the pupil stated that the number of pieces increases by consecutive whole numbers?

Testing hypotheses

Has the pupil tested her ideas by drawing a sketch for a different number of cuts?

Big cheese

A shopkeeper is cutting up a large piece of cheese and she notices that if she makes two cuts she gets 3 pieces:

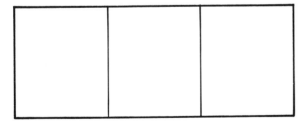

She then realises that if she cuts it like this she will get 4 pieces:

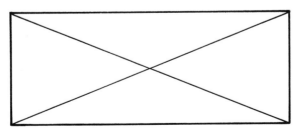

1. What is the maximum number of pieces 3 straight cuts would produce? (The pieces of cheese do not have to be equal in size)

2. What is the maximum number of pieces with 4 straight cuts?

3. What is the maximum number of pieces with 9 cuts?

▶ Is there a pattern which you could describe, which would help you find a general formula for n cuts?

Teachers' notes

Introduction

Pupils shuffle a pack of eight cards, numbered from 1 to 8, using a specified method, and record how many moves it takes to return to the original order. They then repeat the process with more cards, and look at the way one card moves to help predict the number of moves needed for any size pack.

   This activity is suitable for pupils working in pairs or individually. No preliminary knowledge is needed, and the task is suitable for use with upper secondary pupils.

Equipment

Card, scissors.

Running the investigation

Pupils should be encouraged to use the cards until they are confident enough to work without them. Most pupils should be able to follow the instructions and spot the patterns. The more able may notice the connection between modular arithmetic and the number of moves.

Possible extensions

What happens with an odd number of cards?

For 6, 9, 12, 15, etc, what happens with 3 piles?

There are connections between card shuffles and bell-ringing; e.g. Plain Bob:

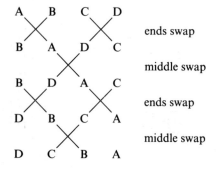

ends swap

middle swap

ends swap

middle swap

Looking at the rules that bell-ringers use could be the basis of an extended piece of work by some pupils.

Answers

1   6 shuffles

Here is the chart for 8 cards, showing the 'path' taken by card 1.

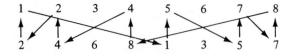

10 cards need 10 shuffles
12 cards need 12 shuffles
14 cards need 4 shuffles.

Assessment

Comprehension

Has the pupil understood how to carry out the shuffle?

Planning

Has the pupil listed all the results of her shuffles?

Searching for patterns

Has the pupil plotted the movement of one card?

Generalising

Has the pupil discovered that if there is an even number of cards p then a card in the nth position goes to $n/2$ if n is even, or to $\frac{1}{2}p+\frac{1}{2}(n+1)$ if n is odd?

Big deal

► Take eight cards numbered 1 to 8 and put them in order.

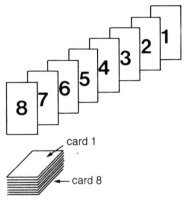

► Make a pile with the cards face down like this:

card 1
← card 8

► Write down the order of the cards:

top   bottom
   1 2 3 4 5 6 7 8

► Deal the cards into two piles face up:

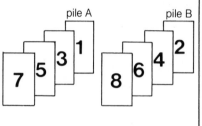

pile A   pile B

► Turn the piles over.

► Put pile B on top of pile A.

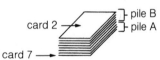

card 2 →   ⎱ pile B
                        ⎰ pile A
card 7 →

► Record the order again:

top   bottom
   2 4 6 8 1 3 5 7

► Repeat the last four steps. Keep doing this until the cards are back in their original order.

top   bottom
   1 2 3 4 5 6 7 8

1.   How many shuffles does it take to get back to the original order?

► Try the investigation again using an even number of cards.

Teachers' notes

Introduction

Suitable for middle to upper secondary pupils. Pupils can tackle the task individually or in pairs. It is likely to take one session of teaching time. No prior knowledge is needed. We have found that it stimulates lively discussion, and helps to develop spatial awareness and the ability to find sequences.

Equipment

Multilink or centicubes. Squared paper.

Running the investigation

A very short introduction is all that is necessary, but you may need to emphasize that only the outer surfaces have labels struck on them. Many pupils will find it easier if they make models of the cubes.

Answers

	1		2		3	
	3 labels	8	3 labels	8	3 labels	8
	2 labels	12	2 labels	24	2 labels	36
	1 label	6	1 label	24	1 label	54
	0 label	1	0 label	8	0 label	27

The general formula for an $n \times n \times n$ cube:

8 boxes have 3 labels
$12(n-2)$ boxes have 2 labels
$6(n-2)^2$ boxes have 1 label
$(n-2)^3$ boxes have no labels.

Assessment

Comprehension

Has the pupil realised that boxes inside the cube have no labels?

Planning

Has the pupil marked the model or diagram to help him see how many labels are on a box?

Searching for patterns

Has the pupil systematically built and dismantled the model (or obtained the answer by counting using a diagram) to see how many boxes are in a particular category?
Has the pupil tabulated her results?

Generalising

Has the pupil stated that 8 boxes have 3 labels for any sized cube?
Has the pupil stated that the number of boxes with 2 labels is a multiple of 12?
Has the pupil stated that the number of boxes with 1 label is a multiple of 6?
Has the pupil stated that the number of boxes with no labels is a cube number?
Has the pupil found the algebraic formulae?

Testing hypotheses

Has the pupil tried his hypothesis with a different size cube?
Has the pupil checked her formulae by adding them up to produce n^3?

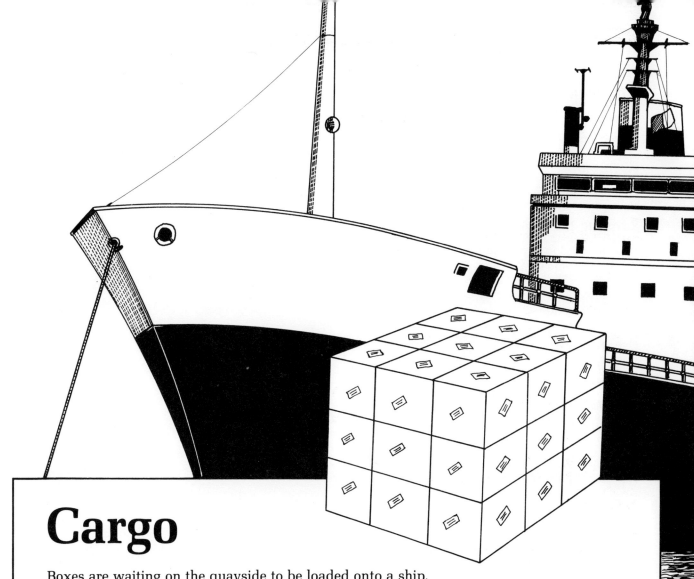

Cargo

Boxes are waiting on the quayside to be loaded onto a ship.

27 boxes are made up into a 3 × 3 × 3 cube like this ready for the crane.

The dockers stick labels as shown on each of the 6 exposed faces of the cube.

The cube is dropped as it is being loaded, and the boxes are scattered.

1. How many boxes have got 3 labels on them?

    How many boxes have got 2 labels?

    How many boxes have got 1 label on?

    How many boxes have got no labels on?

2. Investigate the same problem if boxes are made up into a 4 × 4 × 4 cube.

3. What about a 5 × 5 × 5 cube?

> ►Can you find a general rule for predicting how many boxes will have 3 labels, 2 labels, 1 label and no label, for any size cube?

Teachers' notes

Introduction

Suitable for lower secondary pupils. This investigation gives useful practice in number bonds and recognising prime numbers. Pupils have produced interesting posters showing the cycles of each number.

Equipment

Paper (possibly large, for display).

Running the investigation

You may need to check that pupils understand the rule of subtracting the smaller from the larger and doubling the smaller number. You may also need to ensure that they try every possible number pair for a given number.

Assessment

Comprehension

Has the pupil followed the rules for subtracting and doubling?
Has the pupil looked at all the possible number pairs for a given number?

Searching for patterns

Has the pupil recognised that some cycles are subsets of previous cycles?

Generalising

Has the pupil stated that if a number is not prime, it has more than one cycle? (N.B. the converse is not true, e.g. 17 has two cycles).
Has the pupil noticed that each pair add up to the number?

Presenting results

Has the pupil found a way to present his results showing how cycles can link up, e.g. . . .

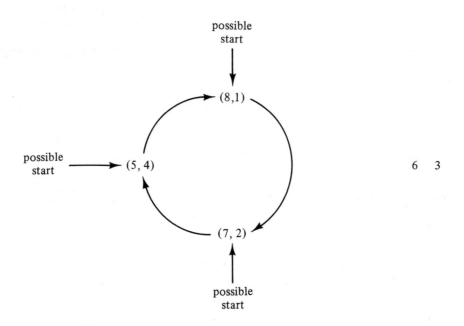

All the possibilities for 9.

CYCLES

9 can be split up as $5 + 4$

These rules are then applied to 5 and 4:

(5, 4)

Take smaller number from the larger	1	8	Double the smaller number
Take smaller number from the larger	7	2	Double the smaller number
Take smaller number from the larger	5	4	Double the smaller number

The cycle is now complete.

Try other pairs of numbers which add up to 9, and find their cycles.

Using these rules, find out what happens with number pairs which add up to 2, 3, 4, 5, 6, 7 ... etc.

►Find a way to display your results, showing the patterns you have found. *What do you notice?*

Teachers' notes

Introduction

Suitable for middle to upper school pupils. This investigation produces interesting number patterns, and is suitable for group or individual work.

Equipment

Calculators!

Running the investigation

A short introduction to repeating decimals may be needed. It should be stressed that many examples with the same divisor need to be tried for a pattern to emerge. To cut down on the calculations required, pupils could work in groups and decide amongst themselves how they are going to apportion the tasks. However, they will need to collect together their results in order to see what happens with a particular divisor.

Assessment

Planning

Has the pupil tried a large number of fractions with the same denominator?

Searching for patterns

Has the pupil collected her results in a systematic way?

Generalising

Has the pupil noticed that 7 has a cyclic pattern?
Has the pupil noticed that the repetend for 11 is related to the 9 times table?
Has the pupil noticed that the reciprocal of $999\ldots9$ (n times) is

$$0 \cdot \underbrace{00000\ldots01}_{n-1}\underbrace{0000\ldots01}_{n-1}\underbrace{00\ldots\ldots01}_{n-1}\ldots?$$

Presenting results

Has the pupil presented the results of his investigation in a clear and concise manner?

Decimal  Patterns

123/9 = 13·666 ... The repeating digit 6 could be called the REPETEND

Sometimes the REPETEND is a series of digits.
For example, 123/99 = 1·242424 ...

Use your calculator to work out other fractions in a decimal form. Try dividing with 5, 7, 11 ...
Then use other odd numbers as divisors.

Can you see any patterns?

Write down the repetends for each decimal fraction.

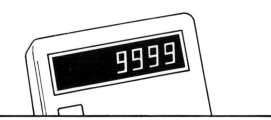

▶ Further investigate what happens when any digit is divided by any member of the set 9, 99, 999, 9999, ...

Try other sets of numbers a, aa, aaa, aaaa ...

Describe the patterns you get.

Teachers' notes

Introduction

This is suitable for lower secondary school pupils. No prior knowledge is needed. Most pupils will successfully complete this investigation and will explain the patterns verbally; some will be able to do so algebraically. It could be used as an introduction to investigations.

Equipment

Dice; possibly card and scissors.

Running the investigation

After pupils have answered questions **1** and **2**, it is a valuable exercise to get them to make their own cube, which can be marked as a die. This will involve them working out the net of a cube and where to place the dots. Pupils will need to keep careful records of the results they get in questions **3** and **4**. A proof of the result for the addition of totals involves the fact that the top number is added four times, and each of the four visible side faces is added twice. If the visible sides are thought of as four pairs of opposite faces (sum 7) then their sum can be seen to be 28.

Possible extensions

Can you predict which number sums and number products are possible simply by using the net of the cube?

Find out about dice with other shapes and investigate any number patterns you can find on them.

Answers

1 4.
2 Opposite faces add to 7.
3 If k is the number on the top face, the total is $4k + 28$.
4 Sum of products is $49k$.

Assessment

Comprehension

Has the pupil kept a fixed number on the top face?

Planning

Has the pupil found all the number sums possible with a fixed top number?
Has the pupil considered all six possible top numbers?

Searching for patterns

Has the pupil tabulated or listed her results?

Generalising

Has the pupil stated that sums increase by 4?
Has the pupil found the formula for the sums?
Has the pupil stated that the sum of the products increases by 49?
Has the pupil found the formula for the sums of the products?

Testing hypotheses and proving results

Has the pupil proved the formula for the sum?

Presenting results

Has the pupil produced a clear report with good diagrams and tables?

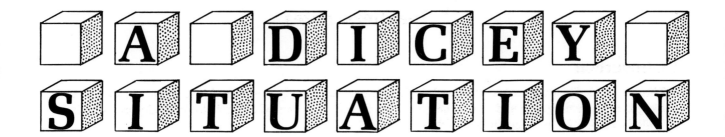

Roll a die until you get the number 3 on the top.

1. What number is hidden, face down on the table?

Repeat this with other numbers.

2. What do you notice about the numbers on the
    opposite faces of the die?

Add the numbers which are visible on the above dice;
e.g. $1+2+3=6$, $1+3+5=9$, ...

Then add these totals. $6+9+ \ldots + \ldots$

Now choose another number. Keep it on the top of the
die, and find the sum of the numbers which are visible, as
before. Find the overall total as before.

3. Continue this process for all 6 numbers on the die.
    What do you notice?

4. Keep the number on the top fixed, as before. But, this
    time, multiply together the visible numbers and add
    the totals. Investigate what happens when you repeat
    this for all 6 numbers.

Teachers' notes

Introduction

Suitable for middle to upper secondary pupils. It is likely to take about one session of teaching time. Familiarity with triangle numbers will help in finding the formula, but it is not essential as this investigation is within the reach of pupils of most abilities.

Equipment

Nothing special needed.

Running the investigation

A short while after giving out the investigation it will be useful to discuss as a class their answers to questions **1** and **2**.

Possible extensions

Pupils should look at what happens if the lift is allowed to go down as well as up, but stopping at a floor only once.

Answers

1   4 moves.
2   2 moves.
For n floors the number of moves is 2^{n-1}.

Assessment

Comprehension
Has the pupil considered all the possible routes to the third floor?

Planning
Has the pupil drawn diagrams or listed routes?

Searching for patterns
Has the pupil looked at buildings whose sizes increase consecutively?

Generalising
Has the pupil recognised how the pattern is formed?
Has the pupil obtained the general formula?

Testing hypotheses
Has the pupil tried his formula for different, new, values of n?

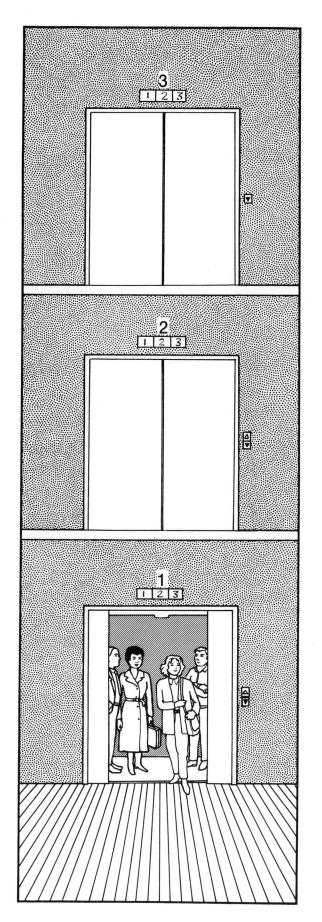

Elevator moves

The lift is programmed to reach the 3rd floor of the building. It does so by various combinations of routes.

For example, a direct route to the top without stopping would be one route—stopping at every floor would be another route.

1. How many ways are there to reach the 3rd floor from the ground floor (not shown in the diagram) if the lift only moves in an upward direction?

2. The 3rd floor is closed for repairs. How many ways are there for the lift to reach the 2nd floor from the ground floor?

▶ Investigate for taller buildings.

▶ What about the lift in the 'mathematical building' with *n* floors?

Teachers' notes

Introduction

Suitable for middle to upper secondary pupils. The first part is relatively easy, the second requires more thought and careful counting.

Equipment

Isometric paper.

Running the investigation

An explanation of why there are more than four triangles in B may be needed. Working in pairs will help with the counting and checking of triangles in the second part of the investigation.

Possible extensions

Calculate the number of squares on a chess board.

How many diamonds are there in a box junction at a road intersection?

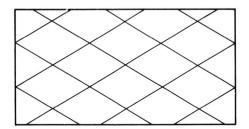

Answers

1 A 1, B 3, C 5
2 Number of triangles $= 2r - 1$.
3 A 1, B 5, C 13

Pattern is

	Number of $n \times n$ Δ's						
Size of Δ	6×6	5×5	4×4	3×3	2×2	1×1	Total
1×1						1	1
2×2					1	4	5
3×3				1	3	9	13
4×4			1	3	7	16	27
5×5		1	3	6	13	25	48
6×6	1	3	6	11	21	36	78

Assessment

Comprehension

Has the pupil counted the 'inverted' triangles in the given triangles?
Has the pupil counted all the possible sizes of equilateral triangles in a given triangle?

Planning

Has the pupil collected her results in an ordered way?

Searching for patterns

Has the pupil tabulated his results in a way that makes the sequences clear?

Generalising

Has the pupil obtained the formula $2r - 1$?
Has the pupil noticed that the number of 1×1 triangles is a square number?
Has the pupil noticed that the number of $n \times n$ triangles is 1?
Has the pupil noticed the other sequences in the table, e.g. the number of 2×2 triangles is

$$\sum_{r=1}^{n} n-r + \sum_{r=1}^{n-2} n-2-r \quad \text{or} \quad 2\sum_{r=1}^{n-3} r+2n-3 \quad \text{for } n \geqslant 3.$$

Expanding Equilaterals

 A

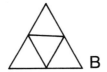 B

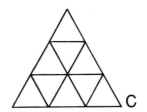 C

1. How many triangles are in the bottom row of A? B? C?

2. If we continue the pattern, can you predict how many triangles there will be in the bottom row of a triangle with *r* rows?

3. How many equilateral triangles are there in A?

   B? (It is not 4!)
   C?

► Investigate how the pattern continues as the equilateral triangle keeps growing.

Teachers' notes

Introduction

Suitable for middle to upper secondary pupils. Pupils will need to be able to recognise perfect squares and understand multiples. Initially pupils should work on their own, but working in pairs may be helpful during the later stages of the investigation.

Equipment

Squared paper would be useful.

Running the investigation

Once the pupils have spent some time looking at the investigation and formulating their approach, it may be helpful to bring the group together to discuss their various approaches.

Most pupils will work on a smaller model of the situation. A useful approach is:

etc.

Possible extensions

Pupils may wish to solve this investigation with a computer, and this is a reasonably easy task.

Answers

1   The lights which are on have an odd number of factors (including 1 and itself). If the number has an even number of factors, the light will be off. So, the lights which are on have numbers which are perfect squares.
2   The formula for finding the number of lights on is $\text{INT}\sqrt{n}$; the number of lights off is $n - \text{INT}\sqrt{n}$.

Assessment

Comprehension

Has the pupil understood which lights should be switched on and off?

Planning

Has the pupil successfully used a model with a smaller number of lights?
Has the pupil attempted to set out her results in tabular form?

Generalising

Has the pupil recognised the final pattern of lights on as the square numbers (or, has the pupil recognised that lights with an odd number of factors will be on)?
Has the pupil formulated his results algebraically?

Testing hypotheses and proving results

Has the pupil tested the results she obtained from a smaller number of lights?
Has the pupil explained the patterns he obtained either orally or in writing?

Flickering Lights

A seaside town has just invested in 1000 new lights to illuminate the pier. They are numbered from 1 to 1000, and linked to a computerised system which can turn on and off any single light.

The pier manager decides to experiment with the system and sets the computer to turn the lights on and off using 1000 computer programs in the following way:

The first program switches all the lights on.

The second program then switches off all the even numbered lights.

The third program will *change the state* of all the lights whose numbers are multiples of three (i.e. if they are off, it turns them on, and vice versa).

The fourth program will change the state of all the lights whose numbers are multiples of 4.

And so on ...

1. *Which* lights will be on after the lights have been subjected to the 1000 different programs?
    Hint: it will probably be easier to work on a model using smaller numbers first.

2. After the manager's experiment how many lights will be on? And how many will be off?

Teachers' notes

Introduction

This task is suitable for lower secondary pupils, and is likely to take longer than one period.

Equipment

Calculators and 100-square grids would be useful, but are not essential.

Running the investigation

If your pupils have already met triangle numbers, then the first part of the investigation will need no explanation. Otherwise, some guidance might be needed.

You may notice that trapezium numbers can be thought of as triangle numbers and parallelograms, e.g.

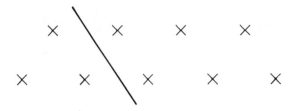

and this can help to find them very quickly.

Possible extensions

For a given number how many triangular or trapezium configurations does it have?

Answers

1 1, 3, 6, 10, 15, 21, 28, 36, 45, 55, 66, 78, 91.
2 5.
3 5, 7, 9, 11, 12, 13, 14, 15, ..., 96, 97, 98, 99, 100.
4 From the final investigative part, the numbers left are 2, 4, 8, 16, 32, 64; i.e. the powers of 2.

Assessment

Comprehension

Has the pupil followed the rules for triangle numbers?
Has the pupil followed the rules for trapezium numbers?

Planning

Has the pupil followed a regular procedure for finding trapezium numbers; e.g. finding the numbers with two rows, then the numbers with 3 rows, etc?

Searching for patterns

Has the pupil drawn diagrams to help him illustrate the patterns?

Generalising

Has the pupil stated that the non-triangle and non-trapezium numbers are powers of 2, or used an equivalent phrase?
Has the pupil stated that the difference of two triangle numbers is a trapezium number, as long as the difference is at least 5?

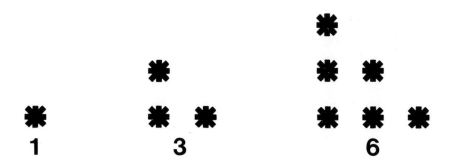

1, 3, 6 are TRIANGLE NUMBERS

1. Find all the triangle numbers smaller than 100.

9 is a TRAPEZIUM NUMBER.

If a number is a trapezium number, it must obey these rules:

(a) there must be at least two rows

(b) each row must be bigger than 1

(c) each row must be one bigger than the row before it.

2. What is the first trapezium number?

3. Find all the trapezium numbers smaller than 100.

4. Which numbers smaller than 100 cannot be drawn as triangle numbers or as trapezium numbers?

What do you notice?

Teachers' notes

Introduction

This investigation is most suitable for fifth year pupils or above. Pupils should work either in pairs or in small groups. It is a useful investigation prior to work on summing series and generalising formulae, and would also be useful at sixth form level.

Equipment

This task is best attempted by drawing diagrams but it might be useful to build 3-D models especially to demonstrate the situation with a small number of towns. Pinboards and elastic bands can also be useful.

Running the investigation

Clearly as the number of towns increases the pattern will become more complex. At this stage it would benefit the pupils to discuss their ideas. Some pupils will use their knowledge of symmetry to good effect by displaying the towns in a symmetric way and recognising the pattern structure. This can be neatly found if the towns are drawn in concentric rings.

Good discussion can take place when pupils consider the case for an odd or even number of towns. This part of the investigation could be well attempted by even the weaker pupils. However, to be able to formulate a general result, pupils will need to have a good grasp of algebra.

Answers

6 towns need 3 flyovers
7 towns need 9 flyovers
8 towns need 18 flyovers
9 towns need 36 flyovers

Assessment

Comprehension

Has the pupil realised that the number of roads leaving a town is one less than the number of towns?

Planning

Has the pupil placed the towns in a symmetrical way (a good example being concentric rings)?

Searching for patterns

Has the pupil recognised that odd and even numbers of towns produce different patterns?

Generalising

Has the pupil produced either or both of these formulae?

n even $\frac{1}{64}[n(n-2)^2(n-4)]$ flyovers n odd $\frac{1}{64}[(n-1)^2(n-3)^2]$ flyovers

Has the pupil recognised that when n is odd, the number of flyovers is a perfect square?

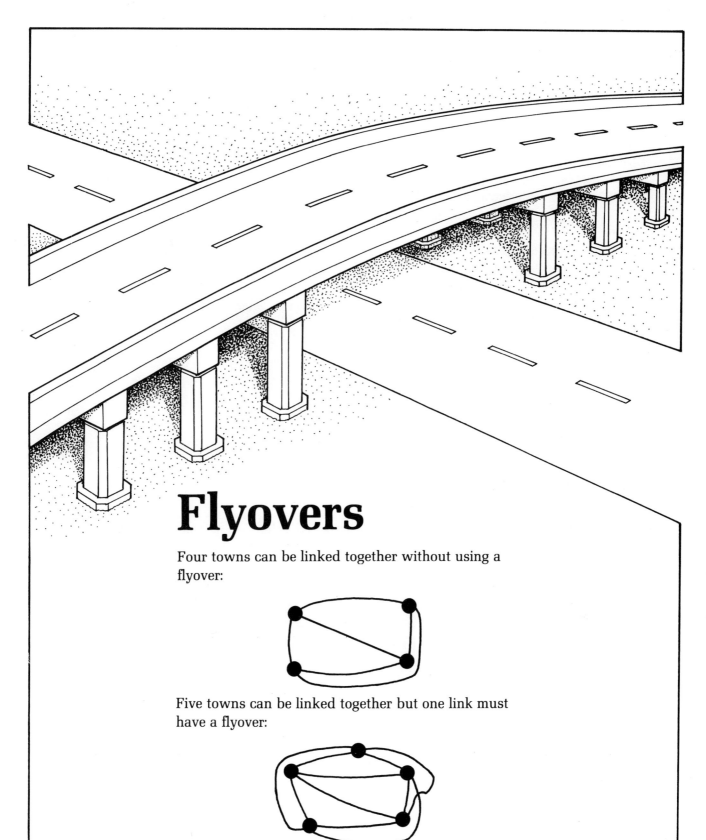

Flyovers

Four towns can be linked together without using a flyover:

Five towns can be linked together but one link must have a flyover:

All flyovers must be separate, with no multi-level junctions.

> ▶ Investigate the smallest number of flyovers needed to link together 6, 7, ... towns.

Teachers' notes

Introduction

Suitable for younger pupils, who need to be familiar with right angles. Pupils could work in pairs on this task to discuss and compare the many possible routes. This investigation is relatively simple and most pupils should get good results. Used with first year pupils, this task would be useful for teachers as a starting point for investigational work, by discussing with pupils the approaches they can use and the things they should look for and develop.

Equipment

Squared paper, tracing paper (useful when finding routes of the piping).

Running the investigation

To save time, it helps if the pupils draw one copy of the estate and then try their routes on tracing paper. You may need to explain how the lengths are measured, with a house being one unit long or wide. Pupils will need to follow the instructions carefully, discuss strategy, and tabulate their results.

Possible extensions

Pupils could investigate the effects of varying the starting and finishing points of the piping, and comparing these results with their original answers. As this is a simple introduction to investigations, it gives the pupils the opportunity to change the rules of the task and design their own rules.

Another extension could be to allow pipes to come off the main pipe at any angle, and to look at the number of turns involved.

Answers

1 3×3 grid needs a pipe 20 units long
2 $4 \times 4 \ldots 28$
   $5 \times 5 \ldots 48$
   $6 \times 6 \ldots 60$
   $7 \times 7 \ldots 76$
3 Odd and even numbers have different patterns:

Assessment

Comprehension

Has the pupil shown one continuous pipe, with no doubling back?
Has the pupil shown pipes into the houses at right angles to the main pipe?
Has the pupil's pipe started and finished at the same point?

Planning

Has the pupil used one part of the pipe to serve houses on both sides of the street?
Has the pupil tried to improve on her results?

Searching for patterns

Has the pupil used the similar pipe patterns from one layout to help with larger layouts?
Has the pupil tabulated his results?

Presenting results

Has the pupil drawn clear diagrams showing the shortest route?

Gas piping

Starting and finishing at the same point in the top left hand corner, gas piping has to pass outside each house.

The piping cannot go back along any part of the route where it has already been laid.

The pipe into the house is at right angles to the main pipe.

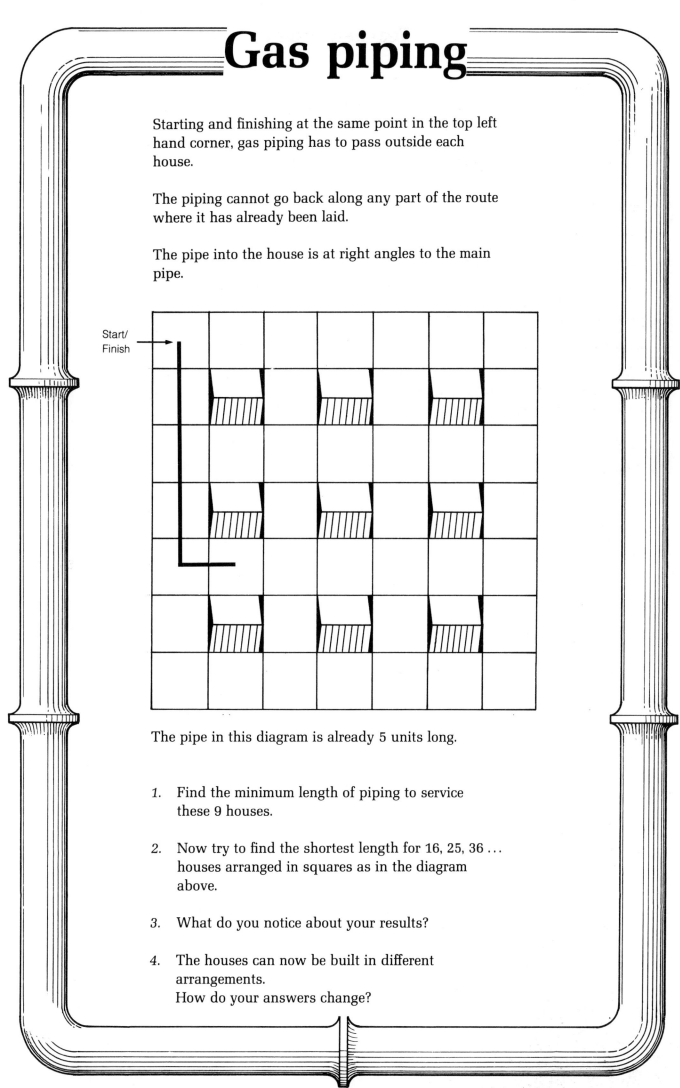

Start/Finish

The pipe in this diagram is already 5 units long.

1. Find the minimum length of piping to service these 9 houses.

2. Now try to find the shortest length for 16, 25, 36 ... houses arranged in squares as in the diagram above.

3. What do you notice about your results?

4. The houses can now be built in different arrangements.
   How do your answers change?

Teachers' notes

Introduction

This task is intended for middle/upper secondary pupils. Its purpose is twofold — first it allows pupils to work with vectors and decide which vector is needed for a certain direction. An element of strategy is also involved. However, the main purpose of this task is to introduce pupils to the idea of developing and designing games which use mathematics and are fun to play.

To understand the game pupils should have knowledge of vector addition, multiplication by a scalar, and finding the magnitude of a vector.

Equipment

Square paper, dice, rulers.

Running the investigation

It would be wise to go through the rules of the game and set any other ground rules you think are necessary. Pupils may work in pairs or teams of two. You may decide to allow pupils to design the layout of the 'first hole' themselves and set their own constraints of bunker, water, and out of bounds areas. This task could be used either as a means of consolidating vector work or used as an investigational way into vectors for the pupils.

Finally, it is important that they are encouraged to change the game, as this will alert them to some of the pitfalls when they design their own game.

Some pupils may need help as to what area of mathematics to use in their games. Approached carefully, this task would be suitable as an extended piece of project work.

Assessment of pupil's own game

In this case, the normal assessment framework is not appropriate, particularly because it is difficult to predict the games pupils will produce! However, these are the areas which should be looked at in assessing the games.

1 What is the goal of the game — can you tell when you have won?
2 Are the rules clear, concise, unambiguous and comprehensive?
3 Has the pupil tried to build in an element of strategy?
4 Can this game be played for a reasonable length of time?
5 Is the game well presented?
6 Is the game worth playing more than once?
7 Is it likely to develop mathematical thinking?

Hit and miss

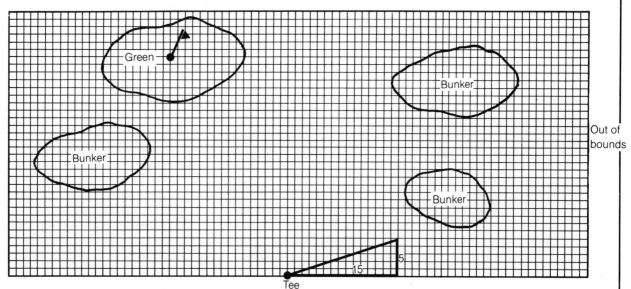

This is a game for two players.

The object is to hit a ball from the tee so that it ends up on the green.

Each player takes it in turn to roll two dice.

The numbers on the dice are used to make a vector, e.g. if you roll 3, 1, this could make the following vectors:

$$\begin{pmatrix} 3 \\ 1 \end{pmatrix} \begin{pmatrix} -3 \\ 1 \end{pmatrix} \begin{pmatrix} 3 \\ -1 \end{pmatrix} \begin{pmatrix} -3 \\ -1 \end{pmatrix} \begin{pmatrix} 1 \\ 3 \end{pmatrix} \begin{pmatrix} -1 \\ 3 \end{pmatrix} \begin{pmatrix} 1 \\ -3 \end{pmatrix} \begin{pmatrix} -1 \\ -3 \end{pmatrix}$$

The choice is yours!

Each time you can use any one of 4 golf clubs to play the shot. Their weightings are 7, 5, 3 and 1;

e.g. if you use 5 and you choose the vector $\begin{pmatrix} 3 \\ 1 \end{pmatrix}$ The ball would move $5\begin{pmatrix} 3 \\ 1 \end{pmatrix} = \begin{pmatrix} 15 \\ 5 \end{pmatrix}$

If your ball goes in a bunker or out of bounds you miss a turn and go back to your last position.

The winner is the person who takes fewer shots to reach the green.

Play the game several times with a friend and keep a record of your moves.

Think of how you could change the game.

Could you make it more … simple … complicated … unpredictable … mathematical?

Write down and discuss your ideas.

▶Now design your own game.
   Write clear rules so that you and your friends could play it.

Teachers' notes

Introduction

Suitable for upper secondary pupils. Pupils should be familiar with trigonometric ratios, the sine rule, and angle properties of polygons and circles.

This investigation will be particularly useful in consolidating the above mathematics. Most pupils will be able to find the ratios of a variety of polygons but only the very able pupils will manage to generalise for an n-sided polygon.

Equipment

Compasses, ruler, and calculator.

Running the investigation

Pupils should be allowed to work on the investigation in pairs so as to encourage discussion and to work collectively on a variety of regular polygons.

At the end of the first session on this investigation, it will be useful to bring the group together in order to share their initial results and to look at the various approaches to the problem. This is an important aspect of consolidation and review of previous work on the mathematics being used.

Possible extensions

Try other regular polygons inside and outside circles.

Can you find the ratio of their lengths?

Answers

1 (a) The length of the equilateral triangle inside the circle is $\sqrt{3}\,r$ where r is the radius of the circle.
   (b) The length of the equilateral triangle outside the circle is $2\sqrt{3}\,r$.
   The ratio of the lengths of the two triangles is 2:1.
   The ratio of the successive areas is 4:1.

For squares in circles the ratio of lengths is $\sqrt{2}$:1, the ratio of areas is 2:1.

For the extension, the ratio is

$$\frac{L_m}{L_{m-1}} = \sec\left(\frac{180}{n}\right), \qquad \text{so} \qquad L_m = L_0 \sec^m\left(\frac{180}{n}\right)$$

where L_m is the length of the mth n-sided polygon.

Assessment

Comprehension

Has the pupil continued the sequence of triangle, circle, triangle, etc correctly?

Searching for patterns

Has the pupil drawn a good sketch with the angles marked on it?
Has the pupil tried to use trig. ratios or the sine rule?
Has the pupil defined the radius of the initial circle?

Generalising

Has the pupil found that the ratio of the lengths is 2:1 and that the ratio of the areas is 4:1?

Testing hypotheses and proving results

If the pupil has found the results by measuring, has she proved it by using trigonometry?

Inside Outside

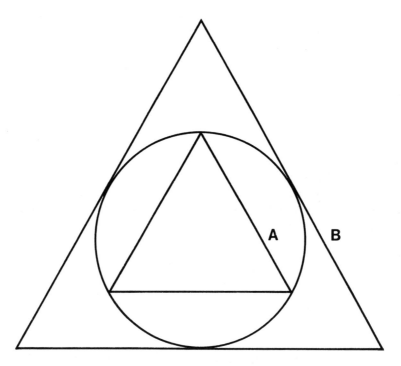

The diagram shows 2 equilateral triangles.

Triangle A is inside the circle

Triangle B is outside the circle

1. What is the ratio of the lengths of the sides of the two triangles?

Continue the sequence of triangle, circle, triangle, circle, ...

2. Find the ratios of the sides as before. What do you notice?

▶ Investigate the areas of successive triangles in this sequence.

Teachers' notes

Introduction

This is designed to be a fairly realistic simulation. It is suitable for middle secondary pupils who are familiar with Pythagoras' Theorem and with rounding numbers to a required degree of accuracy. The second question involves a large number of calculations, and would be best done in groups to share out the workload. It is likely to take a couple of sessions.

Equipment

Squared paper, calculator.

Running the investigation

It should be emphasised that the proposed sites are in the middle of the squares, as is Stewarton.

Possible extensions

Ask the pupils to consider what would happen if the company knew that the price at which they sell the gas is to increase in the future.

Answers

1   α 529035 β 480777 γ 480777 δ 467082 ε 445000 Ω 509202 (all thousand pounds).
2   $\alpha, \gamma, \Omega, \beta, \delta, \varepsilon$ (by using the ratio of return: cost).
3   Stewarton$\rightarrow\varepsilon\rightarrow\delta\rightarrow\beta\rightarrow\Omega\rightarrow\alpha\rightarrow\gamma\rightarrow$ Stewarton   266·3 miles.

Assessment

Comprehension

Has the pupil realised that the cost of the rig is constant and does not affect the relative cost of developing the sites?
Has the pupil realised that he has to calculate the distance of the rig from Stewarton?

Planning

Has the pupil used Pythagoras' theorem to *calculate* the distance of each field from Stewarton?
Has the pupil found the costs of development simply by *measuring* on a scale diagram?
Has the pupil rounded her answers to the nearest £1000?

Generalising

Has the pupil used a reasonable method (e.g. return: cost) to find the order of development?

Presenting results

Does the pupil's report show clearly the order of development with reasons for the final recommendations?

It's a gas

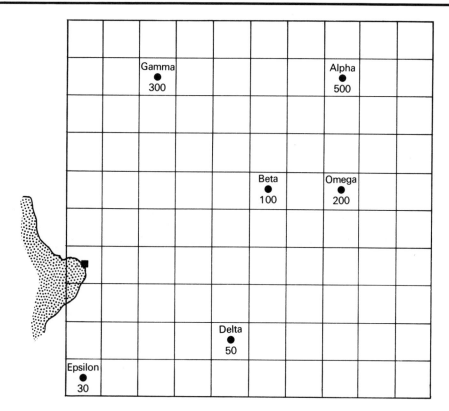

The U.K.G. gas company has won licences to develop 6 sites in the North Sea. The locations and sizes of the gas fields, in millions of cubic ft of gas, are shown above.

Stewarton is the site of the storage depot, to which pipelines are to be laid. The costs involved are:

pipeline   £1·5 million per mile
   rig   £400 million for each site.

U.K.G. only develops one site at a time, so a new site is not started until the old one is exhausted.

1.   What is the cost of developing each site, correct to the nearest thousand pounds?

2.   In what order should the sites be developed in order to get the highest profits first?

After the sites are exhausted, U.K.G. has to make sure the sites are secure and safe.

3.   A security boat from Stewarton visits each rig in turn. What is the shortest route it could take on its tour of the rigs?

Teachers' notes

Introduction

Suitable for lower school pupils. The investigation is likely to take about one period of teaching time. It should help to develop pupils' abilities to recognise the relative size of numbers and will give useful practice in calculation skills. The rule for finding the greatest product is not immediately obvious but it is well within the capabilities of most pupils.

Equipment

Calculators.

Running the investigation

Pupils can start this investigation without any introduction needed, but you might find it useful to discuss with the whole group their initial result for four digits.

Some pupils feel sure they have found the biggest product when in fact they have not, and you will need to suggest they try more examples. On some calculators, pupils will fairly quickly encounter numbers in standard form and you will need to explain what is happening.

Possible extension

Suppose you were given the opposite problem — what is the smallest product you could make using the above set of digits?

Answers

1 $41 \times 32 = 1312$
2 $63 \times 54 = 3402$
3 $93 \times 85 = 7905$
4 $964 \times 8753 = 8\,437\,892$

Assessment

Comprehension

Has the pupil realised that he can use the digits once only?
Is there evidence that the pupil has recognised the relative size of numbers?

Planning

Is there evidence that the pupil has tried all the combinations of the digits?
Has the pupil found the largest product with six digits before trying seven digits, etc?

Searching for patterns

Has the pupil tried to identify by inspection the pattern for the largest product (either written or verbal evidence)?

Generalising

Has the pupil found the rule for any number of digits; i.e., for A B C D E F in descending order, $ADF \times BCE$.

Little and large

Using the digits 1 2 3 4
we use each of the digits once only to make a product
e.g.
 1 2 × 4 3 = 516

1. What is the biggest product you can make by using the digits?

2. What is the biggest product you can make with the digits 3 4 5 6?

3. What is the biggest product using the digits 3 5 8 9?

▶ Try finding the biggest product with 5 digits. All five digits must be different.

▶ Investigate what happens with more digits.

4. If you have spotted a pattern, you should be able to find the biggest product using the digits 9 8 7 6 5 4 3.

Teachers' notes

Introduction

This investigation is suitable for lower secondary pupils and does not require prior knowledge. However, the extension material is more suitable for older or more able pupils. Most pupils find this task very enjoyable and often compete to be the first to produce correct solutions. Pupils usually work on a trial and error basis at first, but quickly recognise the pattern which helps them solve the triangle.

Equipment

Calculators could be made available, but this is a good exercise for developing mental calculations. Sets of magic triangle diagrams would be helpful.

Running the investigation

Pupils should work individually and be encouraged to record their results carefully, looking for patterns. They should see the relationship between the vertex sum and the sum of the sides.

   Please note that solutions for triangles with sides totalling 18 and 22 are not possible — this could be explored further as a supplementary activity.

Assessment

Comprehension

Has the pupil used each digit once only?
Has the pupil found the right totals?

Planning

Did the pupil show evidence of building on her initial attempts?
Did the pupil devise a method for finding all possibilities? E.g. for 'sum 9' the vertices must be 1,2,3; for 'sum 10' vertices are 1,3,5 only; etc.

Searching for patterns

Did the pupil tabulate the results of the correct sequence and recognise the significance of the sum of the vertex numbers?

Generalising

Has the pupil recognised that as the sum of the sides increases by 1, the sum of the vertex numbers increases by 3?
Has the pupil stated the formula

$(\text{sum of sides} - 7) \times 3 = \text{sum of vertices}$?

MAGIC TRIANGLES

Using the numbers 1, 2, 3, 4, 5 and 6, fill in the circles
so that the sum along each side is equal to the
number given below the diagram. Each digit can be
used only once.

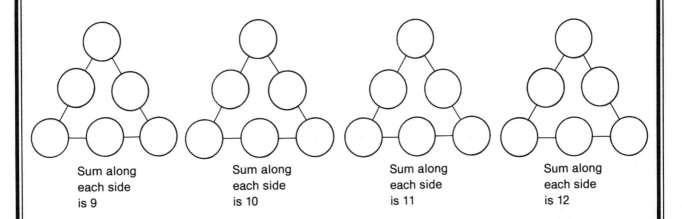

Sum along
each side
is 9

Sum along
each side
is 10

Sum along
each side
is 11

Sum along
each side
is 12

Can you see a pattern?

▶ Now using the numbers 1, 2, 3, 4, 5, 6, 7, 8
and 9, investigate for triangles with 9 circles.
For example:

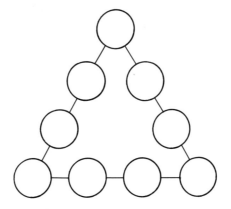

Sum along each side is ... 17, 18, 19, 20, 21, 22
and 23

▶ Investigate further for triangles with 12
circles, using the numbers 1, 2, 3, 4, 5, 6, 7, 8,
9, 10, 11, 12

Teachers' notes

Introduction

This is suitable for upper secondary pupils. Prior knowledge of percentages and money calculations is needed. The first part of the investigation is fairly straightforward, with pupils searching for answers to specific questions, and pupils of all abilities will be able to make some progress.

This investigation is useful for consolidating calculator skills.

Equipment

Calculator.

Running the investigation

You will need to ensure that the pupils understand that the sum of money which is distributed remains £1 m throughout.

Some pupils will find it useful to draw a tree diagram with the amounts of money written on each branch.

Possible extensions

Pupils could use the current bank rate of interest instead of 10%. This might mean that pupils will have to give their answers to 2 d.p. earlier than they have to when the rate is 10%.

A harder extension is to see what happens when a charity keeps a proportion of the profits and passes the rest on with the original amount.

Answers

1   1024 (2^{10})
2   £97·66 to 2 d.p.
3   17 years

Assessment

Comprehension

Has the pupil understood how the money is distributed?

Planning

Has the pupil used a systematic approach to find (a) the distribution of money, (b) the number of charities?
Has the pupil used a different method for distributing the money?

Searching for patterns

Has the pupil tabulated her results?
Has the pupil used a tree diagram?
Has the pupil tried to find out what eventually happens with a different method of distribution?

Generalising

Has the pupil stated that the number of new charities at the beginning of the nth year is 2^n?
Has the pupil stated that after n years the profit is $\frac{1}{10} \times 1\,000\,000/2^n$?

Money grows

A million pounds is left in a will.
The money is to be distributed to charities, but in a
rather unusual way.

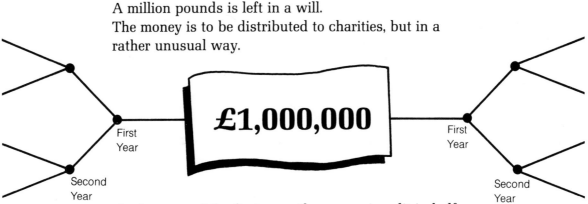

£1,000,000

First Year

Second Year

First Year

Second Year

At the start of the first year, the money is split in half
between two charities, who are allowed to invest the
money and keep the profits.

At the end of the first year, each charity must pass on
its share of the original money, split equally, to two
further charities.

Again, they are allowed to invest the money and keep
the profits.

The money is divided and invested by other charities
in the following years.

The rate of interest is 10%.

1. How many new charities would there be at the
   start of the 10th year?

2. What profits would each of these charities get at
   the end of the 10th year?

3. It is not worth investing the money if the profit is
   less than £1. After how many years does this
   happen?

► What if the money had been shared out
  differently? Investigate further!

Teachers' notes

Introduction

This task is suitable for middle secondary pupils. It involves recognition of the different days on which a year starts, along with the different lengths of a year. It is suitable for individual work, and is likely to take around one session of teaching time.

Equipment

Calendars of past years would be useful.

Running the investigation

Pupils can often be surprisingly vague about the way in which a day in one year becomes the following weekday next year, and may need to be helped to see what is happening by reference to their birthdays. A table or chart to see how the cycle of different years is constructed would be helpful and many will produce this unaided.

Possible extensions

How many Friday 13ths can there be in a year?

What happens in a new century? (Some centuries are leap years, some are not.)

Answers

1   14 (7 ordinary and 7 leap).
2   Occurs in a cycle of 28 years, with e.g. the leap year starting on a Wednesday as follows

1st time (leap)	2nd time	3rd time	4th time	5th time
	5 years later	*6 years later*	*11 years later*	*6 years later*

and the pattern of 6,11,6,5 is the same for different days, although in a different order.

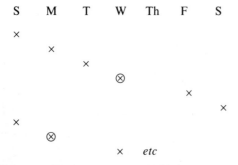

4   Leap years that start on a Wednesday, Thursday or Friday. Non-leap years that start on a Thursday or Friday. In these years there are 53 Fridays.

Assessment

Comprehension

Has the pupil understood how the start day progresses from year to year?
Has the pupil used the leap years?

Searching for patterns

Has the pupil used a chart to see how the years progress?
Has the pupil looked at the gaps between years starting on the same day?

Generalising

Has the pupil listed the cycle of years starting on the same day, i.e. 11,6 (leap), 5, 6?

Name the day

The year shown here starts on a Sunday, and is not a leap year.

The next year starts on a Monday and *is* a leap year.

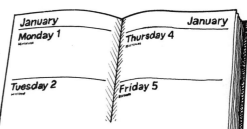

The following year starts on a Wednesday and is not a leap year.

So these are all examples of different 'types' of year.

1. How many different types of year are there?

Find a way to illustrate how the different types of year occur.

2. How often does each one occur?

▶Do you notice any patterns?

3. On what day does your birthday fall this year? Can you predict on what day it will fall in 10 years time?

4. Suppose you were paid every Friday. Which years would give you the most pay days?

Teachers' notes

Introduction

The task is suitable for middle to upper secondary pupils, because although the finding of the number bonds is very simple the analysis of the pattern involved is complex.

Equipment

Nothing special needed.

Running the investigation

This investigation should be done in pairs so that all the combinations can be found and cross-checked. In the early stages, it would be prudent to bring the group together to check their initial answers.

Possible extensions

Write down the number bonds you have found for a particular number, but change them into products:

e.g. $6 = 3+2+1$ as a product $3 \times 2 \times 1 = 6$
$6 = 3+3$ as a product 3×3 $= 9$
$6 = \ldots\ldots$

Find the greatest product for each of your numbers.

Answers

1 For the number 6 there are 10 number bonds.

The number of combinations can be obtained from the table below.

Number to make	Using numbers less than or equal to:								
	1	2	3	4	5	6	7	8	9
1	1	1	1	1	1	1	1	1	1
2	1	2	2	2	2	2	2	2	2
3	1	2	3	3	3	3	3	3	3
4	1	3	4	5	5	5	5	5	5
5	1	3	5	6	7	7	7	7	7
6	1	4	7	9	10	11	11	11	11
7	1	4	8	11	13	14	15	15	15
8	1	5	10	15	18	20	21	22	22
9	1	5	12	18	23	29	31	32	33
10	1	6	14	23	30	35	38	40	41	42

The table was constructed as follows: The number of ways to make the number n using $1, 2, \ldots, m$
$=$ the number of ways to make n using $1, \ldots, m-1$.
$+$ the number of ways to make $n-m$ using $1, \ldots, m$.

Assessment

Comprehension

Has the pupil found all the possible number bonds using just addition?

Planning

Has the pupil written down all the different number bonds in a systematic way?

Searching for patterns

Has the pupil realised that the elements of the combinations for a particular number can be split up using the number bonds he found for the previous numbers?

Communicating results

Has the pupil listed the various combinations in a sensible and clear manner?

Number bonds

Choose a number, for example 6.

Write down all the combinations of numbers which make that number, using only addition

e.g.

$$6=3+2+1$$
$$6=3+1+1+1$$
$$6=...$$

►Investigate

1. How many different combinations of numbers can be used to make up your number?

Now look at other numbers and list how many combinations you can find for each number.

9   5   7   8   11

4   6   12   14

16   10   15   17

Teachers' notes

Introduction

Pupils of all ages and abilities should be able to draw polygonal numbers. Finding the rules for each type of polygonal number may prove harder for many, but they should be able to describe the patterns and continue them.

   This investigation is useful either for introducing polygons or at the conclusion of work on regular shapes, neatly showing the connections between geometry and number patterns.

Equipment

5 cm sq. paper and calculators.

Running the investigation

It should be pointed out to pupils that the first number in any polygonal number is always represented by one dot. After a very brief introduction most pupils will be able to draw the arrays and start to record their results. At this stage it can be useful to bring the group together to discuss the patterns they can detect and to share their ideas before they try to find a formula. Prompt: "Can you explain to me how star numbers are formed?"

The first four star numbers may be written as follows:

$1 = (1 \times 1) + (4 \times 0)$ $8 = (2 \times 2) + (4 \times 1)$
$21 = (3 \times 3) + (4 \times 3)$ $40 = (4 \times 4) + (4 \times 6)$

showing the pattern of a square number plus triangular numbers.

Possible extensions

Pupils could be encouraged to look at the relationship of triangular numbers within each type of polygonal number, e.g. pentagonal and triangular numbers:

$5 = 3 + 1 + 1$

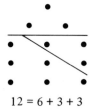
$12 = 6 + 3 + 3$

Pupils could write short computer programs for each type of polygonal number. Here is a listing in BASIC for the first 100 triangular numbers:

```
1Ø   REM THIS PROGRAM LISTS THE FIRST 100 TRIANGULAR NUMBERS
2Ø   FOR I=1 TO 100
3Ø   N=I*(I+1)/2
4Ø   PRINT N
5Ø   NEXT I
6Ø   END
```

Answers

nth star has $3n^2 - 2n$ dots
10th star has 280 dots
15th star has 645 dots
20th star has 1160 dots

Assessment

Comprehension

Has the pupil understood how a star number is formed?

Planning

Has the pupil considered consecutive star numbers?

Searching for patterns

Has the pupil tried to split the star numbers into square numbers and triangular numbers?

Generalising

Has the pupil shown that the nth star number is the nth square number $+ 4 \times (n-1)$th triangular number?
Has the pupil found the formula; i.e. nth star number is $n^2 + 2n(n-1)$?

Testing hypotheses

Has the pupil tested her hypothesis by checking her formula with new star numbers?

Number Configurations

These are the dot patterns of the first three star numbers.

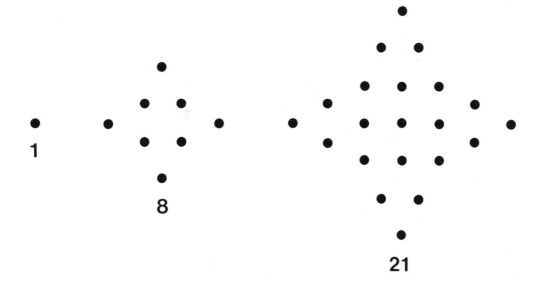

1   8   21

1.   Can you find the next 3 star numbers?

▶ Investigate the pattern of a star number.
Try to find out how many dots are in the 10th, 15th and 20th star numbers.

▶ Now draw some dot patterns for pentagonal, hexagonal and other polygonal numbers.

▶ Can you find a rule for each type of polygonal number you have drawn?

Teachers' notes

Introduction

This is suitable for lower secondary school pupils. The task is a combination of useful practice in mental calculations and finding a simple strategy. The task could be completed by most children in one session.

Equipment

Calculators may be needed for checking.

Running the investigation

All it needs is a simple introduction!

Possible extensions

Compare the total of circles arranged in rectangular patterns of the same area; e.g. 3×4, 6×2.

Answers

1 24 arrangements
2 21, 24, 25
3 For a, b, c, d in ascending order the biggest total is given by the

arrangement $\begin{pmatrix} d & c \\ b & a \end{pmatrix}$ or $\begin{pmatrix} d & b \\ c & a \end{pmatrix}$ or any rotation of these.

Assessment

Comprehension

Has the pupil realised that the numbers can be rearranged?

Searching for patterns

Has the pupil tried to find all the arrangements?
Has the pupil realised that many of the arrangements are rotations of each other?

Generalising

Has the pupil produced the rule for generating the biggest totals?

Presenting results

Has the pupil shown the result in a diagram or communicated it verbally?

The Number Exchange

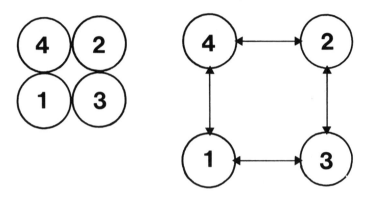

Multiply the numbers in the touching circles and put your answers on the arrows between the circles.

Add up the numbers on the arrows and record the total.

1. How many different arrangements of the numbers are there?

2. What is the total for each arrangement?

3. Which arrangements gave you the biggest total?

▶ Investigate with different numbers in the 2 × 2 circles. What do you notice?

▶ Can you find the biggest total with circles in a 3 × 3 pattern?

Teachers' notes

Introduction

This task can be used to consolidate Pythagoras' Theorem, and so is most suitable for pupils in year 2 or 3 upwards. Pupils will need to be able to find areas of triangles and should know how to square numbers.

   Suitable for individual/group work.

Equipment

Square dotted paper. Possibly pinboard, elastic bands.

Running the investigation

Pupils first have to work out why (1,2) defines the square. Have an overhead projector or other teaching aid ready to explain to those who need it that (a, b) is step a, turn left, step b, all the way round the square. Some will need help in working out the area of the offset square, by subtracting triangles from an enclosing square. Finding the relationship between (a, b) and the area $(a^2 + b^2)$ will prove difficult for some.

Assessment

Comprehension

Has the pupil understood why (a, b) defines the square?

Planning

Has the pupil used sensible 'steps' like (1,3), (1,4), etc to define her offset squares?

Searching for patterns

Has the pupil tabulated or listed his results?

Generalising

Has the pupil arrived at $a^2 + b^2$ for the area of the offset square?

Proving results

Has the pupil shown that the side of the offset square is $\sqrt{a^2 + b^2}$?

Offset Squares

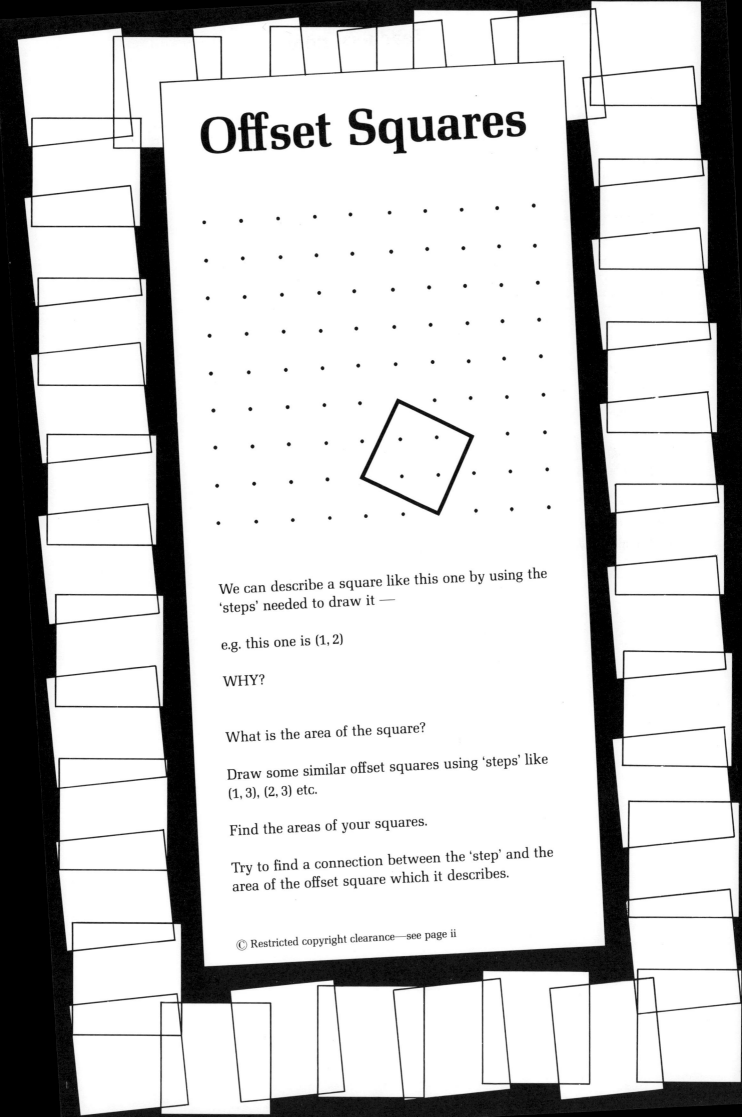

We can describe a square like this one by using the 'steps' needed to draw it —

e.g. this one is (1, 2)

WHY?

What is the area of the square?

Draw some similar offset squares using 'steps' like (1, 3), (2, 3) etc.

Find the areas of your squares.

Try to find a connection between the 'step' and the area of the offset square which it describes.

Teachers' notes

Introduction

Pupils are asked to investigate how much macaroni (or similar) they can hold in an open-ended container, using a sheet of card for the sides and a hard surface for the base. This task is best suited to groups of 2–4 pupils.

The task is equally useful as an introduction to volume and as a task for older pupils with some prior knowledge, although their responses will depend on the extent of that knowledge.

Equipment

Macaroni — allow about 40 cupfuls per group in a central store. Issue as needed.
Card — about 5–10 sheets of the same size per group.
Scissors, sellotape, plastic cups.

Running the investigation

Pupils should work in small groups (2–4 pupils). Many pupils will need a lot of time to experiment. They should be encouraged to record all their results. Measurement in cupfuls should be encouraged. (Some may use units of volume at a later stage.)

Some pupils may spend a lot of time trying different shapes, before considering *cutting up the card*. They should be given the chance to find out for themselves that a rectangular tube contains less than a cylinder of the same height, and that if you reduce the height and thus increase the base area, it will contain more. The maximum volume occurs when the height is equal to the diameter of the pieces of macaroni.

They should be encouraged to discuss their results and the implications for packaging: "Why don't manufacturers use short, broad packets?"

Possible extensions

Some pupils may wish to prove the results. This proof can be fairly simple using the connection between height and area of cross-section. An able or senior pupil might attempt a proof with calculus, although this can be complicated.

When the pattern has been spotted, some pupils may wish to move onto using volume formulae, to calculate the volumes accurately rather than in cupfuls.

Some pupils may wish to write a program to compare the effect of different base areas and different heights.

Answers

1,2 Pupils' answers will depend on the containers they have made.
3 No; they could hold more in a cylindrical store.
4 (a) A low cylinder with a large radius would hold most macaroni.
    (b) It would be difficult to load and unload the grain; and the store would take up too much room.

Assessment

Planning
Has the pupil cut the card to create the shapes?
Has the pupil recorded her results using her own notation or cm^3?

Searching for patterns
Has the pupil attempted to use different shapes?

Generalising
Has the pupil made a statement to the effect that as h decreases, V increases?

Proving results
Has the pupil attempted a proof using $V = \pi r^2 h$ or calculus?

Presenting results
Does the report include an analysis of the implications for packaging?

Packing it in

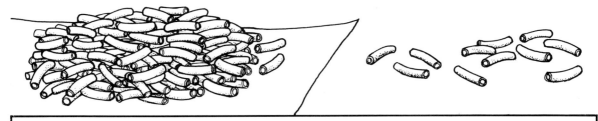

Here is a challenge. You have some macaroni and a piece of card.

▶ Build a container to hold as much macaroni as possible.

▶ You may only use one sheet of card for your container; and the area of each card should stay the same.

▶ Use the floor or a table as the base of your container.

▶ Don't make a lid.

▶ Record your results so that a friend could check them by making the same container.

▶ Try building other containers. Use only one piece of card for each container. Do you get more in?

Use your results to help you answer these questions.

1. What was the greatest amount of macaroni any of your containers held?

2. What was the smallest amount of macaroni any of your containers held?

3. Have the Thetford Grain Company built the best grain store they can with the materials they have? Explain your answer.

4. (a) Explain how you could use the same materials as the Thetford Grain Company to hold **must** macaroni.

   (b) Why aren't real grain stores this shape?

Teachers' notes

Introduction

This is most suitable for lower secondary pupils. No prior knowledge is required but if pupils can recognise sequences it would help. Most pupils enjoy this task, and produce excellent display material.

Equipment

Cm squared paper, isometric paper; use of coloured pens will improve the presentation of the patterns.

Running the investigation

It would be useful to demonstrate the problems on an overhead projector so that pupils fully understand the rules for expansions. Pupils should then work individually but they should be encouraged to discuss any patterns they have found.

Possible extensions

1 Investigate for other shapes.
2 Position three squares centrally in an 11×11 square. How many expansions are needed to cover the square completely?
3 Try to find the number of expansions required to cover other size squares and rectangles.

Answers

For squares the expansion pattern increases in multiples of 4, i.e. if there are s squares in the first expansion, the nth expansion will consist of $s + 4(n + 1)$ squares.

Note that an expression for the nth expansion in terms of the number of squares *initially* depends on the starting pattern.

For the pattern given on the pupil's sheet, the 10th expansion will be 43 squares.

The 15th expansion will be 63 squares.

Assessment

Comprehension

Has the pupil followed the rule consistently?

Planning

Has the pupil positioned the start pattern centrally?

Searching for patterns

Has the pupil tried different starting patterns with 3 squares, 4 squares, triangles and other regular shapes?
Has the pupil tabulated his results?

Generalising

Has the pupil stated that the patterns with squares go up in multiples of 4?
Has the pupil stated that with triangles the pattern alternates 2, 4, 2, 4, . . . ?
Has the pupil found the algebraic formula?

Patchwork Quilt

Start with 3 squares and join them together to form a pattern.

Now draw new squares to touch each edge of the original pattern. These new squares represent the '1st expansion' of the pattern.

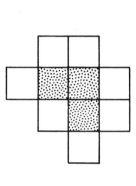 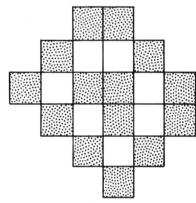

Continue the expansion pattern and count how many squares you add on at each stage.

How many squares would you expect after 10 'expansions', 15, ..., n 'expansions'?

Now, still using 3 squares, try other starting patterns, and make them grow in the same way.

What do you notice?

> ▶ Investigate further, using 4 or more squares with different starting patterns.

What happens if we change the shape and use triangles for our quilt?

How many triangles would you get after 15 'expansions'?

> ▶ Investigate further!

Teachers' notes

Introduction

This is suitable for middle and upper secondary pupils, who will need a sound understanding of symmetry. Suitable for pairs or small groups.

Equipment

Mirrors or mirror card.

Running the investigation

Little if any introduction need be given. Pupils will need time to try examples out. Working in small groups, comparing results, will minimise the possibility of false conclusions. Pupils should be encouraged to make careful sketches, rather than accurate drawings.

Possible extensions

Where possible, pupils should consider the different shapes that can be made with the same number of lines of symmetry; e.g. quadrilateral with one line of symmetry could be:

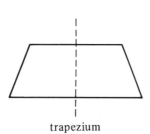

trapezium

arrow head

Answers

1 No   **2** 0, 1, 2, or 4

Assessment

Comprehension

Has the pupil realised that she had to find all the different possible numbers of lines of symmetry for a polygon?

Planning

Has the pupil tried to find if the polygon has more than 1 line of symmetry?

Searching for patterns

Has the pupil listed or tabulated his results in a systematic way?

Generalising

Has the pupil recognised that for a polygon of n sides, n lines of symmetry are always possible?
Has the pupil recognised that for a polygon of n sides, the number of lines of symmetry is given by the factors of n?

Polygon Symmetry

Triangles can have ...

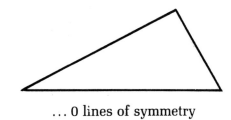

... 0 lines of symmetry

... 1 line of symmetry

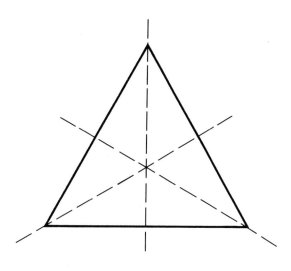

... 3 lines of symmetry

1. Can you draw a triangle with 2 lines of symmetry?

2. How many lines of symmetry can quadrilaterals have?

▶ What about other shapes? INVESTIGATE the number of lines of symmetry which are possible for other polygons.

Teachers' notes

Introduction

All ages, 11 to 16 years can tackle this investigation. No prior knowledge is required. It is designed to help develop spatial awareness. Pupils will benefit by working in pairs or small groups on this investigation. This will allow pupils to discuss their ideas, and pupils of different abilities can work together.

Equipment

Squared paper, scissors. Pinboards, elastic bands, multi-link or centicubes would be useful.

Running the investigation

Some pupils may prefer to cut out the 'tables and spaces', while others may prefer to use a pinboard, or multi-link on squared paper. It will help if pupils collate and tabulate their findings as they go along.

Pupils will recognise the patterns which different positions of table produce, and the effect on the number of seated people.

Possible extensions

After pupils have considered different square areas, they could then consider different shaped rooms having the same areas. Alternatively, they could vary the size and number of tables, and compare results with previous findings.

Assessment

Comprehension

Has the pupil included at least two tables of each type?
Has the pupil left the required space between tables, and between tables and the walls?

Planning

Has the pupil minimised the space between tables by overlapping the spaces left around them?
Has the pupil tried to improve upon previous attempts by varying the approach; e.g. by using more large tables, using more small tables, etc?

Restaurant Tables

The crosses represent people sitting at restaurant tables in the following positions:

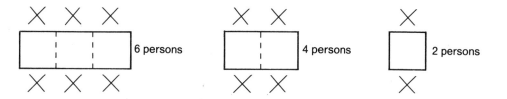

Using at *least two* of each type of table,

▶INVESTIGATE the maximum number of people that can be seated in a restaurant with a floor area of 11 units by 11 units.

A gap of at least one square must be left between groups of diners and the restaurant walls as shown by the shaded areas in the example.

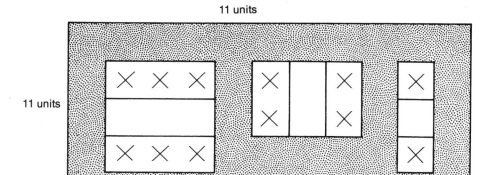

▶INVESTIGATE further the maximum number of people who can be seated in areas of

    13 by 13 units

    14 by 14 units

    15 by 15 units

    $n \times n$ units

Teachers' notes

Introduction

This investigation is suitable for middle to upper secondary pupils. It is likely to take about one session of teaching time.

Equipment

Paper

Running the investigation

You may need to discuss the fact that two 'exchanges' are need to bring A and B up to date with each other's news. You may also need to suggest to some pupils that they use notation to help record what is happening.

Possible extension

Consider the case when n people get together without any prior discussion; e.g. when 3 people get together the least number of exchanges needed is just 4:

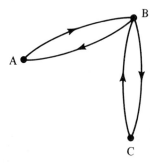

Answers

1 2   **2** (a) 3   (b) 5

Assessment

Comprehension

Has the pupil realised that when A and B are 'up to date' *either* of them can pass on news to a third person?

Planning

Has the pupil devised a notation to help her discover how many exchanges are needed?

Searching for patterns

Has the pupil tabulated or systematically listed his results?

Generalising

Has the pupil stated that if there are n people present, the number of exchanges has increased by n from its previous total?
Has the pupil stated that the number of exchanges is one less than the relevant triangle number?
Has the pupil stated the formula: no. of exchanges $= \frac{1}{2}n(n+1)-1$ [or $\frac{1}{2}(n+2)(n-1)$]?

RUMOUR MACHINE

Before the days of mass-circulation newspapers, news was spread by 'word of mouth'. In the village pub one evening, all the news was being shared — each person was passing on all he or she knew to one other person at a time.

 1 If there are just two people in the pub, how many 'exchanges' are needed so that they each know all the news?

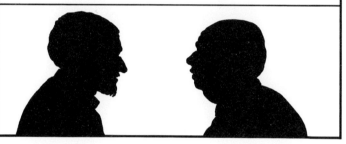

2 A third person joins them.
(a) How many new exchanges happen so that all three know all the news?
(b) So, how many exchanges in total were needed?

▶ More and more people come into the pub. What is the least possible number of exchanges so that everyone is completely up to date on all the possible news? *Assume that every person in the group has the information before it is passed on to another person.*

Teachers' notes

Introduction

This activity is suitable for upper secondary pupils, who need to be familiar with vectors. In it, pupils investigate the mappings which relate the numbers in the squares at each end of ladders and snakes.

The ladders and snakes are moveable, and can be described by vectors, e.g. $\binom{0}{2}$. Pupils can choose their own ladders and snakes to investigate, and need not use those shown on the board.

Equipment

Pupils may need blank copies of the board, or squared paper.

Running the investigation

When you introduce the activity, explain the need for a systematic approach. Very little introduction need be given. There are a variety of directions that pupils can follow, and too specific an introduction may push them all in the same direction. A sensible start for a pupil could involve simplifying the problem:

— taking a vertical vector
— taking the same vector in different positions
— starting from the same number or same row
— looking at odd or even rows

Results need to be carefully tabulated if any generalisations are to be possible.

Possible extensions

Effect of confines of the board.
Use of snakes.

Assessment

Comprehension

Has the pupil understood how a ladder (or snake) is defined by a vector?
Has the pupil understood how a mapping is defined?

Planning

Has the pupil moved the ladder in a systematic way?

Searching for patterns

Has the pupil recorded her mappings in a systematic way?
Has the pupil tabulated his results?

Generalising

Has the pupil tried to generalise her results? E.g. for a vector $\binom{0}{n}$ where n is odd,

$$x \rightarrow 20r + 1 + 10(n-1) - x = x_{r+1} + 10n + x,$$

where r is the row number and x_{r+1} is the number in the box above x.

When n is even, $x \rightarrow 10n + x$.

Snakes and Ladders

In the game of snakes and ladders you try to get from square 1 to square 100. How many squares you move depends on the throw of a die. If you land at the bottom of a ladder you climb to the top of it. If you land on the head of a snake you slide down to the bottom.

The snakes and ladders can be shown as vectors.

The vector for this ladder is $\begin{pmatrix} 2 \\ 6 \end{pmatrix}$

The vector for this snake is $\begin{pmatrix} 2 \\ -5 \end{pmatrix}$

100	99	98	97	96	95	94	93	92	91
81	82	83	84	85	86	87	88	89	90
80	79	78	77	76	75	74	73	72	71
61	62	63	64	65	66	67	68	69	70
60	59	58	57	56	55	54	53	52	51
41	42	43	44	45	46	47	48	49	50
40	39	38	37	36	35	34	33	32	31
21	22	23	24	25	26	27	28	29	30
20	19	18	17	16	15	14	13	12	11
1	2	3	4	5	6	7	8	9	10

If you land on 5 you move to 25.
You can record your move like this: 5→25

> This is called a mapping

► Choose any ladder to investigate.

► You may move it around the board.

► You may not change its length or its slope.
  (So its vector is always the same).

► Plan and carry out an investigation of the mappings you get by moving up your ladder from different squares on the board.

► If you have time, carry on investigating.

Here are some ideas. Try to think of your own ideas to investigate.

★ Move up different ladders from the same square.
★ How about the snakes?

Teachers' notes

Introduction

Suitable for lower to middle secondary pupils. Prior knowledge of perimeter and area needed and for the last part pupils will need to be familiar with the area of a circle.

Equipment

Square dot paper or square cm paper. Calculators will be needed for the last section.

Running the investigation

Only a short introduction should be needed and this can best be done using a pinboard projected on a screen. Pupils should be encouraged to tabulate their results in order to help find a general result.

Pupils could draw a graph of the length of one side of the rectangle against the area, for a fixed perimeter, and this may help them move away from just considering integer lengths.

Answers

1 6·25 sq. m   **2** 9 sq. m

For a rectangle of perimeter p the maximum area occurs for a square of side $\frac{1}{4}p$.

For a fixed perimeter, a circle gives the maximum area.

Assessment

Comprehension

Has the pupil drawn rectangles with the correct perimeter?

Planning

Has the pupil considered different possible dimensions for each rectangle of given perimeter?
Has the pupil considered dimensions in a systematic way, e.g. 1×6, 2×5, etc?

Searching for patterns

Has the pupil listed his results to make pattern spotting easier?

Generalising

Has the pupil stated that the largest area is given by a square?
Has the pupil stated that this square has a side of $\frac{1}{4}p$?
Has the pupil found that the largest area, allowed any shape, is given by a circle?

Presenting results

Has the pupil clearly stated how the miner would gain the maximum benefit from the various proposals?

Gold has been discovered in the Klondyke and to stop arguments among the prospectors, the Government gives each miner the same length of fencing to stake out his claim.

The Government starts by giving everyone 10 m of fencing. This can be cut up in any way the miner wants.

1. The miners decide to enclose rectangular areas. What is the biggest possible area?

Each month the Government gives each miner another 2 m of fence.

2. What is the greatest rectangular area that can be enclosed by 12 m?

> ▶Investigate the largest rectangular area that can be staked out in subsequent months.
>
> ▶Investigate what happens if the miners are allowed to enclose any other shape they like with their fencing.

Teachers' notes

Introduction

This activity is suitable for lower secondary pupils and will help with pattern recognition as well as the relationship between the sides of triangles. It will take at least one session of teaching time. Pupils need no prior knowledge.

Equipment

Geostrips or straws and scissors would be useful.

Running the investigation

Pupils should be given time to explore the situation, to find out, if necessary, that triangles are only possible when the sum of the two smaller sides is greater than the largest side. An explanation using geostrips joined with paper fasteners on the overhead projector can be used to illustrate this concept. As an alternative to strips, pupils could of course construct the triangles using compasses.

Answers

1 Only triangle 2, 3, 4 is possible.   **2**   2 extra — 2, 4, 5 and 3, 4, 5.
The numbers of extra triangles produce the pattern 2, 4, 6, 9, 12, 16, 20, . . .; i.e. the even numbers produce the square numbers; the odd numbers produce a sequence increasing in even steps.
When $n = 1000$, number of extra triangles $= 249\,001$.

Assessment

Comprehension

Has the pupil understood that only certain lengths of sides will produce a triangle?
Has the pupil realised that only the extra triangles are counted each time?

Planning

Has the pupil realised that for each new number she only has to consider those triangles with one side equal to this number?
Has the pupil listed all the possible triangles in a systematic way?

Searching for patterns

Has the pupil considered consecutive numbers of stricks?

Generalising

Has the pupil given the sequences listed above?
Has the pupil stated that the sequence increases in double steps, i.e. 2, 2, 3, 3, 4, 4, etc?

Stick to Triangles

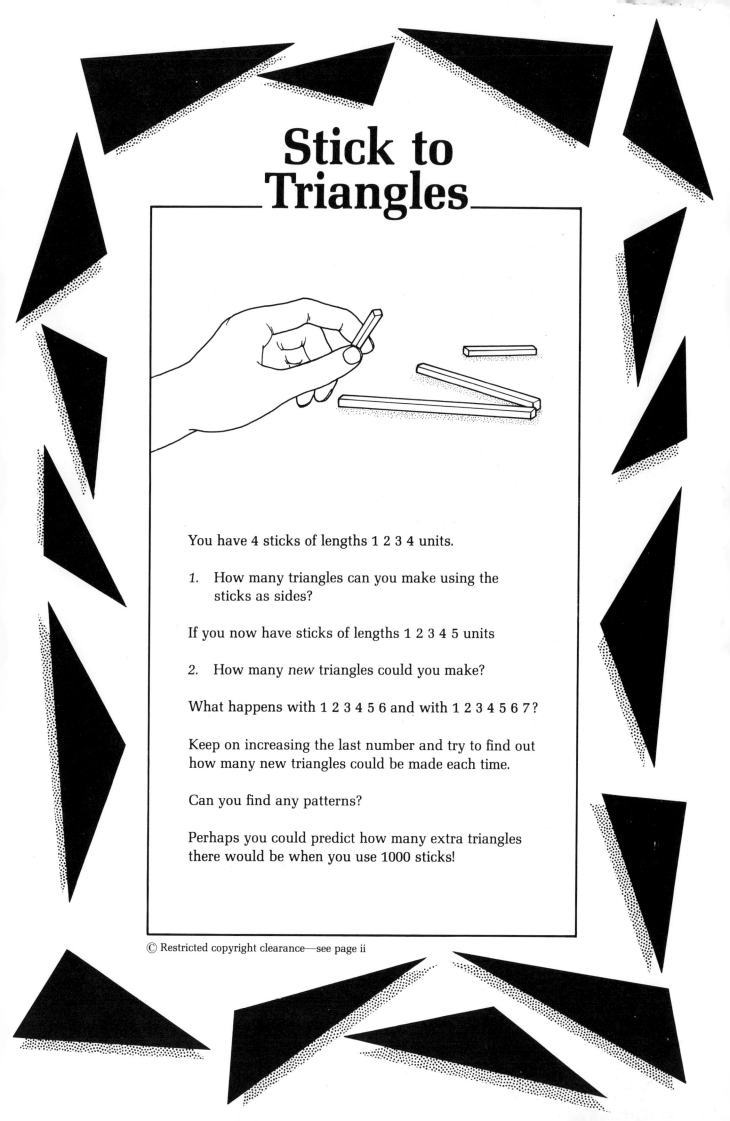

You have 4 sticks of lengths 1 2 3 4 units.

1. How many triangles can you make using the sticks as sides?

If you now have sticks of lengths 1 2 3 4 5 units

2. How many *new* triangles could you make?

What happens with 1 2 3 4 5 6 and with 1 2 3 4 5 6 7?

Keep on increasing the last number and try to find out how many new triangles could be made each time.

Can you find any patterns?

Perhaps you could predict how many extra triangles there would be when you use 1000 sticks!

Teachers' notes

Introduction

Suitable for upper secondary pupils. Prior knowledge of vectors and determinants would be useful, but is not essential. Knowledge of areas of rectangles and triangles is essential.

Equipment

Squared paper.

Running the investigation

A short introduction on the board or overhead projector to remind pupils of vectors might be needed. Allow them to find the answer to question 1 — some may need to be shown that the area can be found by surrounding the triangle with a rectangle and subtracting the areas of the surplus triangles. When the pupils try their own triangles, you will need to ensure that they always start vectors at the origin.

Answers

1 9   **2** 1

If the vectors are $\begin{pmatrix} a \\ b \end{pmatrix}, \begin{pmatrix} c \\ d \end{pmatrix}$ then the area is $\frac{1}{2}|ad-bc|$.

Assessment

Comprehension

Has the pupil started the vectors form the origin?
Has the pupil accurately found the area of the triangles?

Planning

Has the pupil considered the areas of triangles in all four quadrants?
Has the pupil considered triangles where the vertex A is below OB (or below B)?

Searching for patterns

Has the pupil tried to find a connection by manipulating the numbers in the vectors?
Has the pupil tried to find a connection by using letters instead of numbers?

Generalising

Has the pupil found the formula either algebraically or in words?

TANTALISING  TRIANGLES

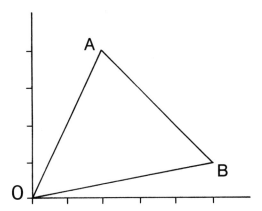

To define this triangle, we use the *vectors* of the lines OA and OB,

i.e. $\begin{pmatrix} 2 \\ 4 \end{pmatrix} \begin{pmatrix} 5 \\ 1 \end{pmatrix}$

1. Find the area of triangle OAB

2. Find the area of a triangle defined by $\begin{pmatrix} 4 \\ 3 \end{pmatrix} \begin{pmatrix} 2 \\ 2 \end{pmatrix}$

> ▶ Draw other triangles using your own vectors. All triangles must have one vertex at the origin.
> Find the area of each of your triangles.
>
> ▶ Investigate the connection between the area of a triangle and the two vectors used to define the triangle.

Teachers' notes

Introduction

Suitable for first year pupils who will enjoy drawing the diagrams. It is a useful introduction to investigations, because of the need for a systematic approach, including tabulating results. Prior knowledge of 45° and reflection would be useful.

Equipment

Squared paper, ruler, coloured pencils, mirrors.

Running the investigation

A short introduction using a transparent grid on an overhead projector would help to emphasise the point about reflections at 45°. You will probably find that even so, you have to check that the pupils' reflections are correct! Pupils should be introduced to the importance of tabulating their results in order to make sense of them.

Possible extensions

Consider the same problem, but with a rectangular grid.

Answers

For a square, any position is possible except the centre and the four corners.

Number of rebounds = 3 from a point on the edge
           = 4 from a point inside

Number of squares passed through = 2 × number of squares on one side.

Assessment

Comprehension

Has the pupil reflected beams at 45° to the sides?

Planning

Has the pupil tried beams leaving Torchy in all four possible directions, where necessary?

Searching for patterns

Has the pupil tabulated his results?

Generalising

Has the pupil found the results listed above?

Presenting results

Has the pupil produced a short account of her observations and how she obtained them?

TORCHY

Torchy positions herself in the corner of a square on the grid and shines her powerful torch.

The torch beam can only move along a diagonal line of 45° and cannot travel back along the same route.

Torchy tries to reflect the beam of light off the sides of the mirrored room so that it eventually shines back on her.

Is it possible?

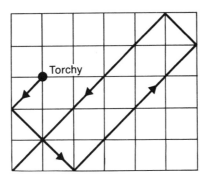

The beam does not shine back on Torchy this time!

What happens if Torchy is moved to different positions?

What is the length of the beam?

How many squares does it pass through?

How many rebounds are there?

▶ Investigate for other grid sizes

Teachers' notes

Introduction

This is suitable for middle secondary school pupils. They will need to know about different solids and how to calculate their volumes. The task will provide useful practice in finding the nets of solids and we have found that pupils enjoy this task and produce very pleasing models for display.

Equipment

A4 card, scissors, rulers, sellotape. Construction materials such as Clixi would also be useful.

Running the investigation

This activity is particularly suitable for group work, where pupils can discuss and refine their ideas. We have found it useful to have books containing nets of solids available for reference.

   We suggest that pupils spend their time initially making rough sketches of the tent and seeing how it can be cut from the piece of card. As well as looking at the usual solids, pupils should be encouraged to use their imaginations and look at unconventional designs.

Possible extension

When this task has been completed, pupils should discuss which shapes produce the least wasted material.

Assessment

Comprehension

Has the pupil constructed his shapes without a base?

Planning

Did the pupil's initial designs give evidence of a planned approach?
Has the pupil produced the correct nets from her initial designs?
Has the pupil worked out the most efficient way of fitting the net on the card?
Has the pupil calculated the volumes of the solids accurately?
Has the pupil shown creativity by considering unusual designs?

Communicating results

Has the pupil produced a report which includes the sketches of the nets, calculation of the volumes and an indication of how the net was placed in the best fit position on the board?

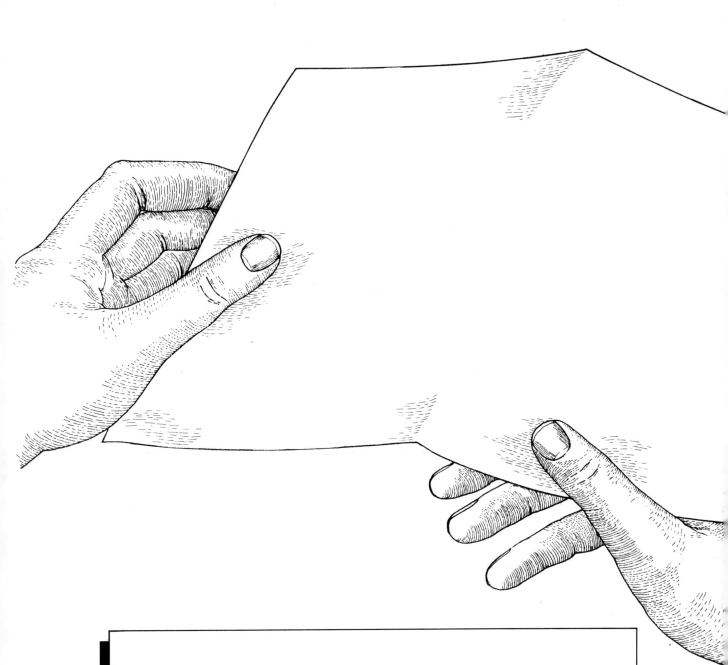

Under Cover

You have a piece of A4 card or paper.
Imagine that the A4 card represents a piece of material which is used to make tents.

Design a tent without a floor covering.

You should be able to make at least 5 different designs by folding and/or cutting 5 pieces of card.

▶Which design of tent has the greatest volume?

Teachers' notes

Introduction

This investigation concerns the patterns which are generated when numbers are added and only the units digit is considered. 'Chains' of digits are produced.

The investigation is best as an individual activity and is appropriate for lower school pupils.

Equipment

Paper.

Running the investigation

A short introduction may be needed to explain 'throwing away' of the tens digit. Pupils will recognise chains and should, hopefully, decide to investigate their lengths.

Some pairs of numbers (e.g. 4, 5) give very long chains but with interesting patterns. Results are ideal for a poster display.

Possible extensions

Similar chains can be generated in many ways (e.g. if a number is even, halve it; if odd, multiply by 3 and add 1). Pupils should be encouraged to try their own rules, and to try writing their own computer programs.

Assessment

Comprehension

Has the pupil always added the last two digits together?
Has the pupil always written down just the units digit of the result?

Planning

Has the pupil realised that if a number pair occurs somewhere in a chain, it is not necessary to investigate separately what happens to that pair?

Searching for patterns

Has the pupil recognised when a chain is complete?

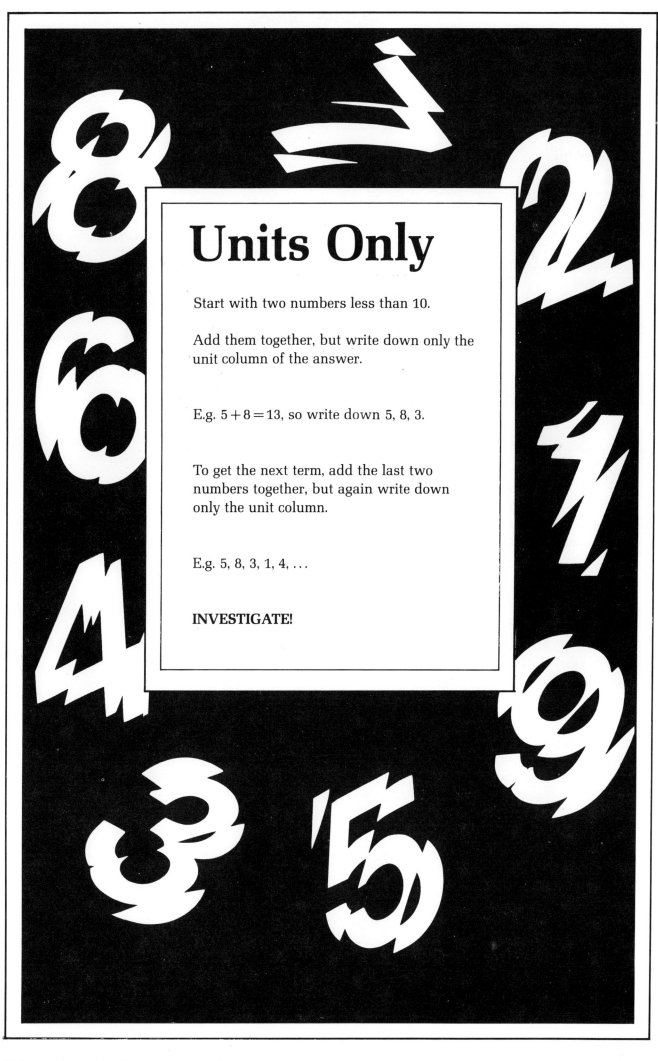

Units Only

Start with two numbers less than 10.

Add them together, but write down only the unit column of the answer.

E.g. $5 + 8 = 13$, so write down 5, 8, 3.

To get the next term, add the last two numbers together, but again write down only the unit column.

E.g. 5, 8, 3, 1, 4, …

INVESTIGATE!

Teachers' notes

Introduction

This is suitable for lower to middle secondary school pupils. Most pupils enjoy this investigation because of the practical activity involved. It will reinforce area and volume work and is intended to show that compact shapes have least surface area.

Equipment

Multilink or centicubes. Possibly isometric paper.

Running the investigation

A short introduction may be required to revise volume and surface area. Better results will be obtained if pupils work in pairs or small groups on this task. For recording purposes, it would help if there were enough multilink for pupils to keep their models; otherwise they will have to record them by drawing and the isometric paper would be best for this. Pupils will need to realise that some shapes are merely rotations or reflections of others and should not be counted twice.

Answers

1 8 shapes
2 16 units
3 18 units
4 See for example *On Being the Right Size and Other Essays* by J. B. S. Haldane (Oxford University Press, 1985).

Assessment

Planning

Has the pupil tried different shapes?
Has the pupil eliminated shapes that are rotations or reflections of others?
Has the pupil recorded the shapes with their surface areas?
Has the pupil recorded the maximum and minimum surface area for each number of cubes?

Searching for patterns

Has the pupil tried a different number of cubes?
Has the pupil tabulated his results efficiently?

Generalising

Has the pupil noticed from her shapes that the minimum surface areas occur when the shape is most compact, and that the maximum surface areas occur when the shape is built with the fewest faces connected?

(Maximum surface area for n cubes $= 6n - 2(n-1)$
$$= 2(2n+1),$$

since there are $6n$ faces and each cube has to touch the face of at least one other cube).

Presenting results

Has the pupil provided a report with carefully chosen examples and explanations?
Has the pupil provided examples of the link between volume and surface area in animals?

Face to face

1. Using 4 cubes how many different shapes can you construct? The cubes must be fitted together face to face.

2. What is the smallest surface area you can find for the shapes?

3. What is the largest surface area?

► Investigate for different numbers of cubes.

► What do you notice?

4. What connection is there between your findings and the way some animals manage to live and survive? Try to find out as much as you can.

Teachers' notes

Introduction

Pupils investigate the movement of a wardrobe around a room, using a grid of squares to represent the room, and a square of card to represent the wardrobe. The investigation is suitable for both individual and group work.

Pupils need some knowledge of simple rotations and 90°. The task may be used to reinforce/enliven work on rotations and other isometric mappings.

Equipment

1 cm or, better, 2 cm squared paper, scissors, rulers.

Running the investigation

To introduce the method of moving the wardrobe, you could use a large cardboard square and a grid drawn on the blackboard or overhead projector. The wardrobe may only be moved by turning it through 90° about a corner. It must start and end its journey with its back against a wall and its handles facing into the room. The handles must not be allowed to touch the wall.

Pupils draw the room plan on squared paper and use a square representing the wardrobe to move about the room. In group work each pupil should try the moves with their own plan and wardrobe.

Encourage pupils to try different routes to the sides of the room, as it may appear impossible to reach some positions (e.g. "try turning your wardrobe in different directions/keeping a different corner on the ground"). When they have discovered that the wardrobe can be moved to any position they can investigate rooms of different sizes, starting with small rooms, and then wardrobes of different sizes.

Possible extensions

Sid needs to move the wardrobe from one corner to the corner diagonally opposite. What is the smallest number of moves he can do this in?

Is the number of moves related to the size of the room?

Assessment

Comprehension

Has the pupil rotated the wardrobe about one corner?

Planning

Has the pupil drawn a careful plan on squared paper and/or used a model wardrobe?
Has the pupil used his own notation to label the wardrobe of plan?

Searching for patterns

Has the pupil used different routes to reach positions at the sides of the room?
Has the pupil tried rooms of a different size?
Has the pupil tried wardrobes of a different size?

The Wardrobe

Here is a plan of a rectangular room.

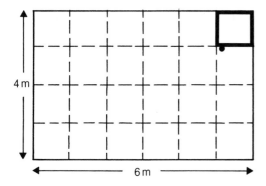

4 m

6 m

In the corner is a heavy wardrobe. Its base is 1 m by 1 m square.

You can only move the wardrobe by keeping one of its corners on the ground and turning it through 90° like this:

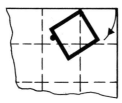

Its back must finish up against a wall. The handle must not touch the wall (it will be damaged). You can't turn the wardrobe through a brick wall!

▶ Investigate whether there are any positions (by the walls) you cannot move your wardrobe to.

▶ Record your results so a friend can check them.

▶ If you have time carry on investigating. Here are some more ideas:

  ★ What about rooms of different sizes?

  ★ What about wardrobes of different sizes?

Teachers' notes

Introduction

This is suitable for middle to upper secondary pupils. Children of all abilities will enjoy this investigation in which they need to explore systematically the problem of allocating the wrong labels to a number of presents.

Equipment

Coloured counters can be used as labels for the sets of presents and this will help pupils to identify the arrangement patterns.

Running the investigation

The first part of this investigation is best attempted through class discussion, as this will help to get the pupils started on the task. We then suggest that the pupils work in small groups.

Possible extensions

Pupils can vary the rule so that one and only one present has the correct label, and these results can be compared with the original task.

Answers

3 presents   2 ways
4 presents   9 ways
5 presents   44 ways
6 presents   265 ways

Extension task: pupils should notice that the number of ways will be the number times that for one fewer present in the original task.

Assessment

Comprehension

Has the pupil realised that *every* present must have the wrong label?

Planning

Has the pupil used equipment or her own notation to make the task easier?
Has the pupil tabulated his results in a systematic way?
Has the pupil explored all the possibilities by keeping one 'label' constant and rotating the rest in an exhaustive manner?

Wrapping Presents

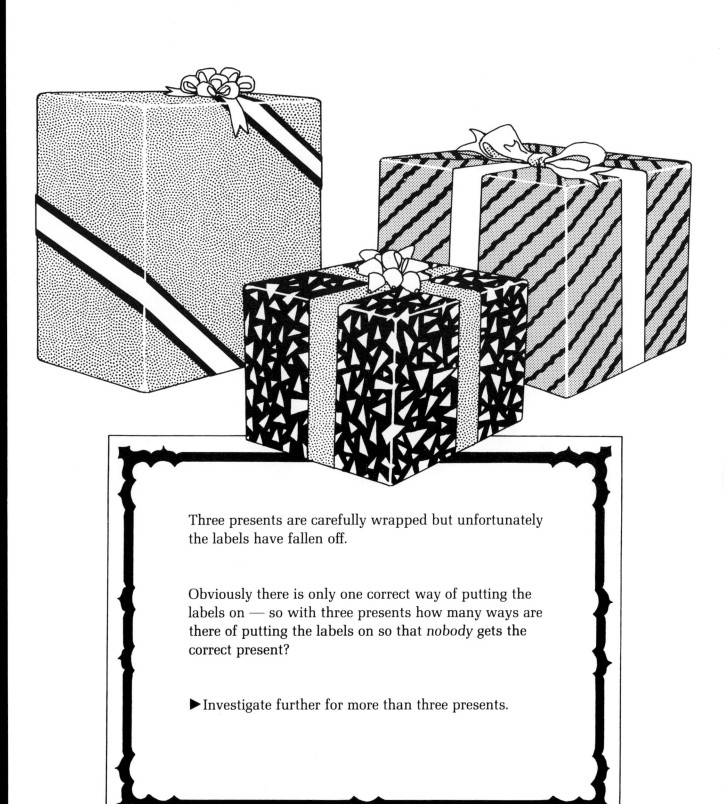

Three presents are carefully wrapped but unfortunately
the labels have fallen off.

Obviously there is only one correct way of putting the
labels on — so with three presents how many ways are
there of putting the labels on so that *nobody* gets the
correct present?

► Investigate further for more than three presents.

Teachers' notes

Introduction

Suitable for middle to upper secondary pupils.

Pupils investigate the number of cubes needed to build ziggurats with different bases. Most pupils should spot the pattern, but only the more able will manage to formulate the results. This is a task in which pupils will be able to work individually at first, but may benefit by working in small groups to formulate their results.

It would be helpful if pupils knew about square numbers.

Equipment

Squared paper, interlocking cubes, isometric paper, coloured pencils. Isometric pinboards and elastic bands might be useful if available.

Running the investigation

Some pupils will need to build models in 3 dimensions, while others will prefer to work in 2 dimensions, using coloured pencils and paper or the pinboard.

Once the patterns have been established it will probably be useful to bring the pupils together in small groups to discuss their findings and work towards a general method. Obtaining the formula, involving the sum of the square numbers, is unlikely for all but the very able!

Possible extensions

Pupils could try drawing ziggurats with rectangular bases rather than the original squares.

Answers

1 14 **2** 30 **3** 140

Assessment

Comprehension

Has the pupil constructed ziggurats with the correct configuration?

Searching for patterns

Has the pupil built several ziggurats or drawn them?
Has the pupil tabulated her results?

Generalising

Has the pupil realised that he has to add the square numbers to get the total number of cubes?

(*Extension*: Has the pupil recognised that for a rectangular base of dimensions $a \times b$, she has to add numbers of the form $a \times b$, $a-1 \times b-1$, $a-2 \times b-2$, etc?)

Testing hypotheses

Has the pupil tested his theory by trying the method with different square bases (*extension*: different rectangular bases)?

Presentation of results

Has the pupil used diagrams or models to show what she has done?

Ziggurats

Ziggurats are towers of stone. They were built by the Babylonians about 4000 years ago.

This ziggurat was built from cubes.
Each layer is a square.
Each layer is smaller than the layer below it.

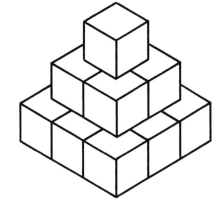

The bottom layer (the base) was built from 9 cubes.
Each side is 3 cubes long, so this is a 3 by 3 layer.

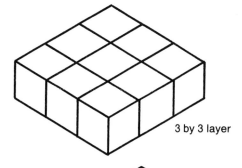

3 by 3 layer

1. How many cubes were used to build the whole ziggurat?

2. How many cubes would you need to build a ziggurat with a bottom layer like this?

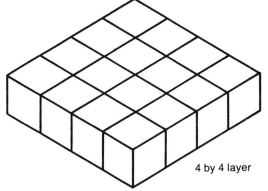

4 by 4 layer

3. How many cubes would you need to build a ziggurat with a 7 by 7 bottom layer?

▶ Investigate how many cubes you need to build ziggurats with other base sizes. Remember: the layers are always squares.

▶ Try to find a way of working out how many cubes you need, without counting them, when you know the base size of a ziggurat.

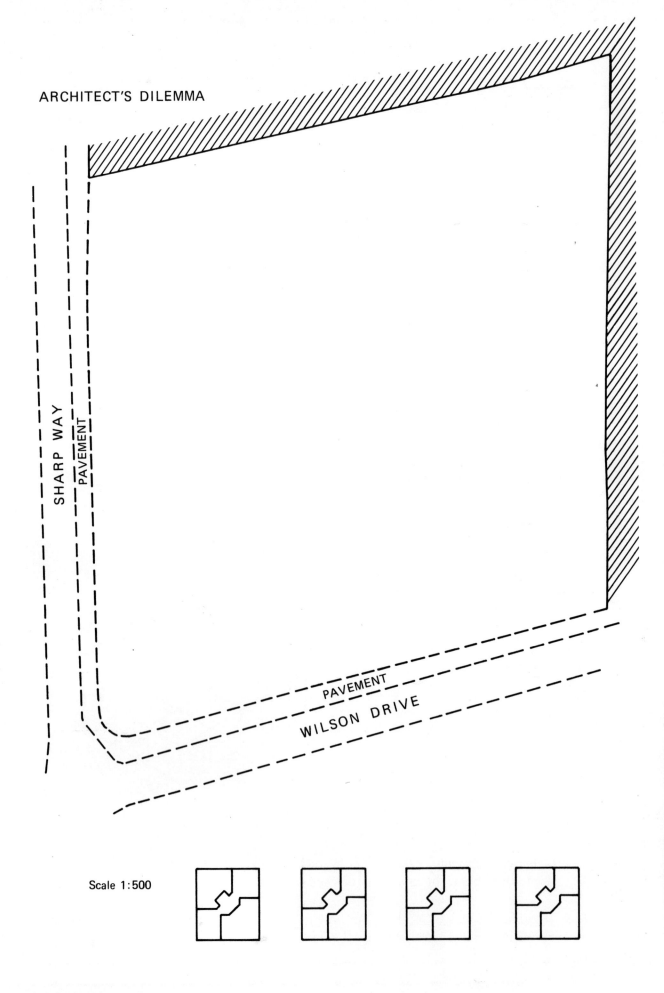

ARCHITECT'S DILEMMA

SHARP WAY

PAVEMENT

PAVEMENT

WILSON DRIVE

Scale 1:500